MW00879458

Today, I Cry No More

Reaping a Harvest from the Tears you Cried

By

Marianela Olivas

1663 LIBERTY DRIVE, SUITE 200
BLOOMINGTON, INDIANA 47403
(800) 839-8640
WWW.AUTHORHOUSE.COM

First published by AuthorHouse 11/24/04

ISBN: 1-4184-9147-0 (sc)

Printed in the United States of America
Bloomington, Indiana

This book is printed on acid-free paper.

Foreword

*B*eing a pastor, I have had the chance to meet and connect with a lot of different people. And there is a very short list of people that have the drive, focus, and passion for life which is alive in Marianela. From the time she came into the ministry she has stayed on a steady increase of growth, wisdom, fun for life and influence. These things make Marianela unique and should make you want to read her book, but there are two main reasons why I think you should read this book.

First, if you lived in the same city as Marianela you would want to be her friend. She is authentic and genuine to all she meets. She has the heart to teach in church in the morning and then graciously offer to drive you home in the same afternoon. She is the type of person that you want to learn from. She reflects the old adage, "What you see is what you get." No pretense. No facades. No masks. She lives life from the heart, which inspires those around her to do the same.

Secondly, this is a book of her life experiences. Some people teach what they know. Some people say what they know. Others live what they know. Marianela is a person who lives what she knows. This trait has given her life much meaning. It is what gives her influence with her peers and superiors and it is one of the reasons this book is going to encourage all who read it.

Writing a book takes a lot of time, effort, and energy. Marianela has taken all of that and more to give to you the thoughts in her heart expressed on paper. From countless hours at coffee shops to late hours in front of the computer, she has done all she can to make this book articulate her heart and soul to you the reader.

If you enjoy the journey of life, the excitement of being a woman, and the value of wisdom, you will enjoy this book, written from Marianela's heart to yours.

Pastor Earl McClellan

Pastor of Singles' Ministry at Shoreline Christian Center, Austin, Texas

Acknowledgements

I would like to dedicate this book to the people who have had the most impact in my life.

The important men in my life, Ricardo Olivas-you made me a wife and mother for that I thank you, Wilfredo Hernandez-you were the love of my life until I realized that hurting so much could not be real love.. I thank you for many, many things. I have forgiven you both and pray that you have forgiven me.

Pastor Robert Koke, Laura Koke, Pastor Earl McClellan, Oneka McClellan, Bishop T.D. Jakes, Bishop Dennis Leonard, Creflo A. Dollar, John Hagee and Michelle McKinney-Hammond thank you for being an inspiration in my life and communicating the word of GOD the way you do, you have all changed me forever.

My beautiful daughters Nichole Alexandria and Bianca Adrianna, you are wonderfully and fearfully made. I am so proud of you. Remember God is the only father you will ever need. Please read this book and use it as a guide to direct you to be the awesome women God purposed you to be.

My future husband Adam Sandoval, the Lord revealed to me that he might bring me a man, but I would not know him as my husband until I was done with the assignment of writing this book and being a testimony and inspiration to other women.. I thank Him for bringing you into my life long before I was done for you to become my best friend. You have made such a difference in my life. Thank you for being such an awesome man of God, for your passion, for showing me what I wanted and needed, most importantly, thank you for teaching me about real love. I love you so much and am very excited about our wedding day, our wedding night, our ministry and the life we will share together.

Lastly, I dedicate this book to my future, knowing that at the end, the life that I will have lived will have been worth it, and I will be able to say that although yesterday I cried, "**Today, I Cry No More**"!

Contents

They that sow in tears shall reap in joy.
Psalm 126:5

Introduction

*M*any, many tears you will cry in this life. Well thank God for those tears for He will direct them to water the fields of your life. Ultimately, the tears you cry will lead you to a harvest that will make everything you live worthwhile. One day you will proclaim '***Today, I Cry No More***".

There is no secret to living life without ever having to cry. Everyone and I do mean EVERYONE has to cry. How do I know? I know because I am downright happy and as one of my favorite writers would put it I am single, sassy and satisfied. Finally, I am reaping a harvest from the tears I cried, and boy have I cried.

I have cried many, many tears in my life. I've cried over poverty, marriage, abuse, divorce, love, betrayal, heartbreak, disappointments, failures and struggles. As you can see my tears have been plenty, but I am here to tell you that I have more than survived. A victim of my tears I've never been, I am victorious and proudly, boastfully, proclaim, "***Today, I Cry No More***". This book is my effort to share lessons I have learned through my experiences and my tears, for it has been through them all and the grace of

God that I have become who I am today, a-better woman, a happy woman, a complete woman.

This book is written for women who have been like me. It is for women who feel like I have felt incomplete and like something is missing. This book is written for women who have had to struggle to break free from the past, who have loved much and been hurt much, and who have had to bury the man who caused them so much. It is for women, who don't yet know how to be women, for women who long to be wives. It is for women who have not yet accepted the Lord, and for those who have. It is written for women who have cried-plenty, yet dare to dream and who long to say, "**Today, I Cry No More**". This book is written for every woman. Men do not be discouraged you love us and desire to know us therefore this book is also written for you.

As a woman who has cried many tears and today cries no more, I tell you, you must trust God, the real love of your life, the king, for He alone can turn your tears of hurt, into tears of great joy.

I remember once hearing that there is a message in your mess, well Praise God for who said that was right. The: Lord blessed my mess and from my misery was born my ministry. Writing this book was instrumental in helping me recover from the biggest hurt, betrayal, pain & disillusion in my life. It is my sincere desire that it be of help to women who are now crying so they too can get to the point where I am today.

In this book, you will learn about many things. You will learn about letting go of the past and getting "him" out of your life. You will learn about the power of forgiveness, that hurt doesn't last forever and that nothing just happens. You will learn about faith and patience, the difference between sex and making love, about being a complete single woman and enjoying the time you have for yourself.

You will learn about being a truly irresistible woman by being both beautiful and spiritual. You will learn about a husband and about being a wife. You will learn about love and marriage, and about the most important thing in your life, the Lord God, a lover of the soul, a lover of the day as well as the night, the one with whom all things are possible. Lastly you will learn about living life to the fullest and about the future that is yet to be.

The lifestyle this book witnesses to is not without it's challenges, or without it's tears. It is not very easy; in fact at times it can be very difficult, yet it is wonderful. It is full of happiness, joy, faith, peace, hope, love and victory. So sit back and relax, or lay back, whatever makes you feel good girlfriend, read, soak it in and apply it. Most importantly, remember that although yesterday you hurt and yesterday you cried, there WILL be a day when you will proclaim *"Today, I Cry No More"!*

1
That Was Then

$\mathcal{U}$nfortunately, many of us have not had the kind of life where we experience God and new birth early in it. We have lived life not knowing right from wrong, sowing bad seed and reaping bad harvest. We have lived life kind of out on a whim, making mistakes at every turn, not knowing that one day we will regret the decisions we made. Many of us, when we find God, make him our Lord, and experience being born again, want to forget our past and put it behind us. We want to forget the choices we made, the things we did, the life we lived, and the people we shared our life with. Just like Jesus called people to be in his ministry that had colorful pasts back then, he calls people with colorful pasts today. As a Christian you are literally a new creation in Christ, the Word says that "the old is gone, the new has come". When it comes to the past, its okay to remember it, and learn from it, what's not okay is to dwell on it. It's good to remember the past for it will remind you of a place where you no longer want to be, a place that allows you to give glory to God. Most importantly remember your past because someday you will use what you learned in it and walk towards your future boldly stating "that was then."

The Beginning from the End

Just as God started the beginning from the end, so did I write the beginning of this book after I was almost done with the end. I had written most of the book, 7 out of 10 chapters and knew what each chapter would be about when I finally started on this, the first chapter.

> *Remember the former things of old; for I am God and there is no other;*
> *I am God and there is no one like me; declaring the end from the beginning and from ancient times things not yet done; saying "My purpose will stand, and I will fulfill my intentions"*
> *Isaiah 46:9-10*

I struggled with this chapter, to the point that thinking about it made me tired, even made me sick. "Why"? You might ask? Let me tell you why. It's quite simple; I didn't want to think about the past. It had taken me so long to get over it; finally my future looked the brightest it had ever looked. I for sure did didn't want to be thinking about the past. Here I was having a strong relationship with God, being a wonderful mother to 2 beautiful, Godly teenage daughters. I looked and felt more beautiful than ever, I had great friends, a wonderful man in my life, a rewarding career, a beautiful home, I was a church leader, a faithful servant, and was looking forward to completing a book that would allow me to be used to glorify God and touch the lives of women all over the world. I was living in purity, and had learned to love the way God loved. My shattered heart had just been put back together again from all the hurt it had been caused. When it came to the past, I wanted nothing more to do with it. I surely didn't want to remember it; what it was like, the things I had done in it, the people who had been in it, especially not the hurt that was caused in it. Interestingly enough, the Lord made me face it and brought me out the way that only he could and through it use me the way that only he could. I began to stand firm on the promise that he wasn't finished with me yet. I was reminded of a song I heard months earlier that ministered to me while I cried a river.

> *You may not understand everything I say or what I do.*
> *You might see my faults and failures and count me out.*
> *You may read the pages of my life and you may wonder*
> *What in earth God saw in me when he brought me out.*
> *But a prisoner of my past I refuse to be.*
> *So I'll stand right here and rest upon his promise,*
> *That what he started he will finish in me!*
> *Wait and see!*

My Story

I would like to share my story with you, before I do, let me first make something very clear. That's that the devil loves to remind us about the good things in our past. Guess why? Because, he wants us back where we use to be, doing what we use to do. He wants to distract us from moving forward and into the Promiseland the Lord has for us. For this reason, he dangles something in front of us to lure us from moving forward. Many times what he dangles in front of us is our past, things we did in it and people in it. Imagine that? That's right! He wants to remind us of the clubs, of the drinking, of the partying, the attention, the wild nights of sex, happy memories with the wrong man that was in your life. Can you feel what I'm saying?

3

Think about it, those were all great things while we were doing them. Think about afterwards—when you woke up the next morning, feeling sick, too tired to get out of bed, feeling dirty, cheap, used, not being treated right by the man you love. God on the other hand, is so different. He reminds us of the bad things so that we will not want to go back there, so that we can move past it. Take note I am not saying he reminds us of the bad things so that we can forget, oh no girlfriend. On the contrary, God wants us to remember where we came from. He wants us to remember so that we can help ourselves and help others. So it happened with my struggle to get started on this chapter, the devil tried to dangle the good things in my life, a sinful, passionate, wild, hurtful relationship with a wrong man. Well, praise God for he delivered me and reminded me how it really was. He reminded me that where I came from—was a place I no longer want to go to.

> *Forgetting what lies behind and straining forward to what lies ahead.*
> *I press on toward the goal for the prize of the heavenly call of God in Christ Jesus.*
> *Philippians 3:13*

I've told you some about how my life in the present, now let me give you some background on how it was in the past. My past goes something like this: it had been a year since my heart had been broken to a thousand pieces by a man I had loved and dedicated my life to for 8 years. It had been almost a year since I'd seen this man and about 8 months since I had even spoken. He, the man who broke my heart was everything to me, we went waaaaaay back, and I do mean waaaaaay back. He was one of my dearest friends for 10 years before we even got together, then he was my best friend, I thought he would always be my friend. Thinking back he really was not my friend, cause let me tell you something, a man, if he doesn't start out being your friend, if he first has sex with you, he cannot then become your friend. Have I lost you yet? You see this man and I had been together at a young age. The fling was short-lived but we remained what I thought was friends for 10 years until we found each other again. Anyway this man was my partner, my confidant, my lover, my cheerleader, my daughters "dad" needless to say, when I lost him, I didn't just lose the man in my life, oh no honey, I lost so much more I wanted to die. It took a very long time for me to get over this man. It was through the grace of God, some things that I will share with you shortly and a very, very special Godly man who became my best friend and this time I knew what was a best friend.   God use this man to show me what I wanted and needed in a man in such a way that in a matter of months I was over the one who had been in my life. I have heard it said that it takes a certain number of years per number of years you were in a relationship to get over it. I am here to tell you that that is a lie from the pit of hell and we can't fall for it. You can get over a relationship, no matter how long it was as soon as you decide to get over it. Anyway, back to the past, I could not think about it without thinking about "him"—the man who had been in my life. I guess you could say that I didn't want to think of the past because deep inside of me I knew there was something I had to face. I mean, I was doing well, I was tough, I was looked up to, but really was I over it? I realized that I had put everything behind me, but still I had not dealt with it. Of course, God is faithful to keep his promise and had to carry on to completion the good work he had began in me and could not until I had dealt with it.

Being confident of this, that he who began a good work in you will Carry it on to completion until the day of Jesus Christ.

Philippians 1:6

It Started with a Dream

Have you ever heard that when God wants you to deal with something, sometimes he won't let you sleep? I mean he is kind and gracious to wake you up in the middle of the night if he has too. Can you feel what I'm saying? I know, because he's done it to me. God with all his wisdom and mysterious ways wanted me to face my past and let me know that by way of a dream. He's so funny. One night when I went to sleep he made me have a dream about "him"- the man that was in my life. A dream that ultimately made me, forget what lied behind and like the scripture said made me strain forward to what laid ahead.

My dream went like this: I dreamed I finally decided to give "him" (the man who had left my life) a call after several months. I was very nervous and wanting to hear the things the devil would want me to hear, things like "What's up babe?", "I've missed you so much", "I still love you", "I want to see you", well guess what I didn't hear any of that, instead, I heard what God wanted me to hear for he wanted to remind me of how it use to be, so what did I hear? "What the h___ do you want?" Wow!!!! Not what I expected. I remember in my dream replying to him very calmly, "You know what, I didn't call you for this" and hanging up. No sooner did I hang up, I woke up. When I woke up, I had this terrible feeling in the pit of my stomach and a migraine that made my head pulsate, I knew right then the Lord was trying to tell me something.

6

The feelings I felt were all too familiar to me and feelings that I had not felt since he had been out of my life. Feelings, I was glad I no longer felt and definitely ones I did not miss. I thanked God for making me face my past and for reminding me of how it used to be, not only that, but also reminding me of what I no longer wanted to feel. That morning while I drove to work, I asked God to forgive me for not letting go of my past, and for him to use me for I had finally faced it and it was behind me. Wouldn't you know, when I got to the office that morning, I had a message, from the Director of my church's Single's Ministry who wanted to see if I could teach Sunday School to the singles at church. Wow!!!! There it was. God had taken me up on my challenge. I prayed and asked him to put in my heart what he wanted me to teach on. He spoke to me to use my facing the past as a lesson. As I continued to pray I kept getting confirmation "Letting Go of the Past…. Letting Go of the Past". The Lord put it in my heart that I was to teach on this for it was an issue that not only I had been struggling with but one that many of my brothers and sisters were also struggling with. I couldn't believe it, just then I actually became excited about my past, to the point, I was looking forward to sharing about it.

But they have conquered him by the blood of the lamb and by the word of their testimony.
Revelation 2:11

Moving Past the Past

The day came when I taught Sunday School, it was one of the most exciting days of my life. It was a day that

God shined through me. That day was all about changing lives and about God. Every bit of it was about God, my being there and speaking, my message, my ministering. The class was very crowded that day, about 60 people. Many of my friends knew I would be teaching and wanted to be there to support me. The special man in my life, my "best friend" was there. The night before, I had gone over the class with him over the phone. He already knew what it was about, but he still wanted to be there to support me and cheer me on. He could tell I was nervous and took me aside and prayed for me before class started, and then sat in the front row to get the best view. Right away when I started speaking, I felt such a calmness overwhelm me; I knew God's presence was there. Everything I said was so real. I spoke so that people could understand and feel what I was saying. There were times when I was so sad I could feel lumps in my throat, you know the ones you feel when you want to cry. There were times when I said things that were so funny I made people laugh. I looked around and saw expressions on faces that let me know everyone was into what I was teaching and it encouraged me. I could see especially see how "my best-friend" marveled at the words that came out of my mouth. He brought such delight to my heart. I respected him so much and had grown so much spiritually since he had entered my life months before, that just a mere look from him was like a "you go girl" and inspired me. I felt that God was right there in the midst of it all, he was smiling at me and letting me know the following:

> *"Well done, thou good and trustworthy slave: thou hast been trustworthy over a few things, I will make you in charge of many things, enter into the joy of your master.*
> *Matthew 25:21*

Okay let's rewind and let me take you back to how I started my teaching. I started by telling everyone that if someone had told me when I started Sunday School a year and a half before, that one day I would be at the pulpit teaching I would have probably busted out laughing, looked at them like crazy and said "Yea Right". I mean that God would use me, I mean it's not like I had a sordid past, but I was no "Miss Goody Two Shoes", I mean I was a mess. I had been married, a victim of abuse, divorced and a single mother, at a very young age. I used, abused and hurt men before they had a chance to use, abuse or hurt me. I didn't have the greatest relationship with my parents. I had been physically, verbally, emotionally and spiritually abused by the men I loved most in my life. I had been betrayed by of the most important man in my life. I had no self-confidence in myself. I did not value myself and walked with my head down facing the ground. "How could God use me?" I asked, very sadly and quietly! I was then silent. Suddenly, I yelled in my oh so sassy New Yorkrican way "Praise God" for he can use anyone and he does"! I mentioned the book that I was writing, and how a lot of what I was going to share came from it, and how my being there in front of them came to be. I told them about the dream.

I got into talking about how to be used by God we first have to let go of the past, second we have to realize our worth and third we have to allow him to use us. My teaching continued like this, I defined the past as being a.) Time gone by; b.) something that happened or was done a long time ago. I gave many examples of things that made up people's past: drugs, alcohol, poverty, rape, molestation, promiscuity, physical abuse, rejection, betrayal, infidelity, divorce, illegitimate children, abortion, and criminal record. After I defined the past, I defined the future, I defined it as a.) A time to come; b.)

what is going to happen later? I gave many examples of this as well: ministry, forgiveness, peace, marriage, children, reconciliation, and victory. I then got into defining feelings: guilt, a feeling of culpability, a sense of inadequacy; unforgiveness: being unable or unwilling to forgive; sensitivity: the capacity of being easily hurt; anxiety: uneasiness of mind, concern; peace: tranquility, state of security; hope: to expect with confidence, a desire with expectation of obtainment. These feelings I explained pretty much can be associated with where you are at, the past or the future. I asked: What feelings do you feel? How do you wake-up feeling in the morning? I stated: Good chance that what you feel is letting you know where you are at!

Let me share with you from my own personal experience about these feelings for I have felt them all. Sadly, many feelings kept me bound and in the past for many, many years. First of all, there was guilt, Wow!!! It's totally amazing how the enemy can use guilt to keep you in the past. I remember during a time of my life when I felt guilty about being happy. Can you imagine that? You see my parents were never happy; they stayed married 17 years for my sisters and me. Never did I see them be affectionate towards each other or show love for one another. The first time I was truly happy, I mean to the point I cried was when I was married, in love with my husband, living in a house for the first time in my life and looking at my newborn daughter Nichole while she slept. I started to cry, my husband looked at me puzzled and asked, "And now what, what's wrong?" I answered him, "it's not fair, I shouldn't be happy, my parents were never happy" I know it sounds crazy but it's what I felt. Finally many years later when I started walking with the Lord, I released myself from guilt and broke any generational curse that had followed my family. I proclaimed in the name of Jesus that I would be happy and that my daughters and their daughters would be happy. Another powerful feeling that will keep you bounded to the past is unforgiveness; we will get into this one in a few. Wow!!!! I continued the class sharing about unforgiveness and how for the longest time it had had a hold on me, and had not let me move past my past. Let's get into another feeling; one I had to be very careful about, that feeling is sensitivity. I was a victim of abuse; I mean I was physically hurt many, many times. Of course, I was very sensitive to being hurt physically, I remember in the beginning of my relationship with the man that broke my heart, we had a heated discussion and I because I was so sensitive to being hurt physically, reacted, by slapping the man, in kind of a "I am not going to take it" fashion. This man up to this point had never touched me, it was the first act of violence in our relationship, in the end, our relationship had become violent. I realized that I could very easily be hurt, I dealt with this feeling by just giving it to God and accepting that my being hurt was in the past. A feeling that got the best of me for a long time was anxiety. I felt this because I knew the kind of man I was with and I did not trust him. After all, I had known him to be a liar and a cheater. How could I trust him? If there's one thing I knew before I really knew the word, was that basic principle? "You reap what you sow". It was because of what I knew about him and the past I couldn't let go of, that even though I knew how much this man loved me and adored me, I never really trusted him, or had peace with him. It was because of the past that I always wondered about him, whereabouts and his doings. When I arrived at the point where I felt no anxiety, instead peace and hope I knew I had let go of the past and was walking towards the future. Peace and hope, wow, that's what you feel when you know God and his promises; it is a sure sign that you have let go of the past.

So what are the past and the future made up of? I asked this question of the class, paused and then started to explain it. The past I said is B.C. in case you haven't heard that before it is "before Christ", the past is yesterday, and made up of three things. There's the devil who represents sin and unrighteousness, there's Judas who represents betrayal, or someone leaving us. How many of you know sometimes we need a Judas in our lives? Of course there's unforgiveness either towards yourself or others. Now, the future that is with Christ, it is today, tomorrow, and is made up of faith, promises, purpose and destiny.

The Power to Forgive

I could not teach on letting go of the past without teaching about forgiveness, for the two go hand in hand. Come on ladies, you got to know that you cannot deal with the past without being able to forgive. Amen! I shared about how I for many years was imprisoned by building bars in my very own heart. Bars that were created by the unforgiveness I carried. I remember holding unforgiveness towards my parents, because they never told me they loved me, because they never told me I was beautiful, because they never told me I was smart and because they never showed me about love. I especially held unforgiveness towards my mother, because she told me I had to get married, even after I told her that I had realized my fiancé was violent and I didn't want to get married. That story by the way was really funny when I taught my class. When I shared it, I shared about my 2 beautiful daughters Nichole and Bianca whom mostly everyone knew. I told them, "when my daughters get marry, since they don't have a father, I'll be walking them down the aisle, and halfway to the alter, I'm going to stop. "I'm going to ask them, are you sure you want to do this?" "If you don't we can turn around and run out of here right now" Everyone went hysterical. Okay, back to unforgiveness, I held unforgiveness towards my ex-husband for not being a good father and not helping me in the least to raise our daughters. As if that wasn't enough, I felt so much unforgiveness towards the man that hurt me and left my life. I had spent 8 years of my life with this man, 8 years, not 8 months now that's a long time, my late twenties till my mid thirties what should should have been the best years of my life. All those years I had carried unforgiveness towards him for the hurt he caused me when he lied to me 10 years earlier when we first got together. You see, I didn't know it, but when we first got together, we were a long way away from home with the military and he was engaged to a woman back home. Imagine trying to have something with a man you've been carrying unforgiveness towards for so long? When he did it again, shortly after we got back together 10 years later, really what I did was compound unforgiveness on top of unforgiveness. That's right he did it to me again. This time we were away again, and he was engaged to another woman far away, where he had been. As if that wasn't enough I now felt unforgiveness towards myself and beat my self up because I should have known better and never let it happen again. "So why did I"? I know you are probably wondering. You know, I loved him and in spite of the lying, the cheating, I thought he loved me, after all, for the second time, I was the other woman, he must have loved me, he couldn't possible love them, I thought.

Anyway, think about your life, your past, things you have not wanted to think about, is there anyone you are holding unforgiveness towards? In Sunday School that day many realized they were holding on to forgiveness. I remember a dear friend who had been raised by her grandmother telling me, "thank your for sharing I am going home right now to call my mother, I have never forgiven her for just leaving me with my grand mom when I was a child and never coming back!" I tell you getting the past behind you at some point will require forgiveness and deliverance. You will never feel healing or see restoration in your life until you forgive. In case you didn't know, it's time you knew that there is incredible power in being able to forgive. Think about yourself. Have you not been forgiven? Remember we were all million-dollar debtors. God showed us his mercy by sending his son Jesus to cancel our debt. Who are we that we cannot extend mercy to others? Believe me you must forgive, if you don't forgive you will answer to God when you get to heaven one day.

> *Then his lord summoned him and said to him, "You wicked slave, as I had mercy on you" And in anger his lord handed him over to be tortured until he would pay his entire debt. So my heavenly Father will also do to every one of you, if you do not forgive your brother or sister from your heart.*
>
> *Matthew 18:32-35*

I finally forgave myself for the unforgiveness I held towards myself, and for not being able to forgive. After I forgave myself, I forgave all the people I had not forgiven in my life. I made a trip home, 1000 miles away to tell my parents that I loved them, and to release them. I really didn't need to do that, the word just says to forgive, however I didn't want something to happen to my parents, never having told them I loved them, and then me not forgiving myself ever. When it came to the men in my life, my ex-husband and ex boyfriend, the one that had really hurt me, well I simply forgave them.

> *For if you forgive others their trespasses, your heavenly Father will also forgive you, but if you do not forgive others, neither will your Father forgive your trespasses.*
> Matthew 6:14-15

Now let me tell you something, I wanted to call them up to tell them, especially my ex boyfriend, the man who had left my life, in fact I wanted to also seek from him forgiveness for there were things he didn't even know I had done, and needed forgiveness for. I didn't though. I didn't because I did not want to open any doors that had been closed. Instead, I gave it all to God. I repented to him and asked for his forgiveness. Let me tell you some things about forgiveness, what it is and what it is not. Forgiveness is to grant pardon for an offense without harboring resentment, it is giving up all rights to seek punishment or retaliation. It is about an act. It's about you repenting to God, and releasing to him what you feel. Forgiveness is beneficial for the person who has been hurt or offended, for it does away with resentment, bitterness, and not letting go of the past. So what is forgiveness not? Forgiveness is not about a response, it does not require remorse or an apology from the person who did the offending.

Forgiveness is not about you forgetting what has been done to you, it does not mean that what happened was okay, and that you automatically trust again and give the offender permission to return to your life as if nothing happened. Forgiveness does not necessarily mean reconciliation but it is the door that opens the way for it. Forgiveness is a process that requires a willing heart and becomes easier to extend as time goes by. What a feeling of peace you feel when you release the prisoner you have held captive in your heart. Forgiveness will give you power and make you feel like you have been set free. Allow no one to be a prisoner in your heart, for if you do, take it from me, you will become imprisoned by it, and that imprisonment my dear sister can be very, very hard.

Let Go & Let God

> *Therefore if any man be in Christ, he is a new creature: old things Are passed away; behold, all things are become new.*
>
> *2 Corinthians 5:17*

Before I ended the class, I talked about "letting go and letting God". There will be a point in your life when you will become so tired of dwelling on the past, looking back at things that are behind you and thinking about what use to be, that you will plea with God to help you find a way to forget about it all. Remember this to forget it does not mean to regret it. It means that you face it and you grow from it. Girlfriend, I am here to tell you that when you get to that point, the only thing you will be able to do about your past is to Let Go and Let God. God wants so much for you to step into the future he has for you, but you first have to let go and leave the past behind you. I've already said it you will never see restoration in your life or feel peace in your mind until you forgive and let go of the things that have hurt you, the people who have hurt you. Let me tell you about that future, it is full of promises that are kept and blessings that are ready to be poured. Walk towards it, towards them. Stop thinking about the past, "that was then", let go of the things and the people that hurt you. Don't let anything or anyone suck the joy out of your life and kill your future. Let God do a new thing in you. Let go and let God, and your life will be renewed, and you will feel an incredible peace.

None of us can change what we have done, who we were, where we have been and to whom we belonged, before we found God. Regardless of the past, understand that God the one who knows your deepest, most shameful secrets loves you and accepts you just the way you are. I challenge you to leave your past in the past, "That Was Then", you are free, and he who the son sets free is free indeed.

In the End

I believe in leaving a class with things that they can apply, in other words not empty handed. So, as I shared with my class, I will now share with you 10 ways to let go of the past and live for the future.

#1 to confess your sins to God and to others.
#2 to forgive yourself and others.
#3 to close any doors that are still open.
#4 to seek first his kingdom and his righteousness.
#5 to rise up when you fall.
#6 to let go and let God.
#7 to turn your misery into your ministry.
#8 to acknowledge that "that was then".
#9 to have a vision and goals and focus on them.
#10 to know God's promises.

I concluded my class with the introduction to this chapter and prayed the prayer that's at the end of it. By the end of my teaching I knew that to teach and speak were my assignment, what I was called to do. I absolutely loved it, it was a blessing to minister to others and to allow God to use things that had happened in my own life to restore lives. I could see that through me, God did something in that room that day that left people feeling different than the way they came in. I saw tears, I saw joy, I saw hope. The praise reports, the accolades, the "I want a copy of that bestseller"!!!!! "Girl, You better autograph my book when I buy it". One of the guys, remembering all the things I never heard from my parents looked me in the eyes and told me "You are beautiful, you are intelligent, and you are loved"!!!!! He made me cry. The emails, the talk for days I loved it all, I just knew that "for such a time as this" was my past, everything I had lived, everything I had suffered, all the tears that I cried.

Final Word

As I stated in the beginning of this chapter, I struggled greatly with writing this chapter. There was something about writing about the past I simply did not want to face. Finally, an opportunity to share on it made me face it and changed everything. I realized that I had lived the past so that I could testify and minister to others. Because of my past I would be a vessel for the Lord. I knew that my past was steering me into the future my heavenly father had purposed me to have.

When I thought of my past and finally faced it, I thanked God for it, and for everything I had lived. I hope that through this chapter I have taught you that God wants you to face whatever you have not been able to face and that he wants to use you and whatever it is you have gone through. My hope is that you being reminded of your past has made you realize that you can use what happened in it to positively influence people's future. My hope is also that you have learned the importance of forgiveness, that you have forgiven yourself and those that you have harbored unforgiveness towards. Lastly, I hope reading what I have written has taught you to let go and trust in God's promises. Most importantly, I hope you have learned to smile about your past thinking "That Was Then!"

Prayer

Heavenly Father, I pray that you will enable me to face my past and that you help me put into correct perspective the things that are behind in my life so that I can move past them and forward to what lies ahead. Let me let go of anything that does not edify me or glorify you. Help me Lord; regard the events in my past as lessons learned in my life. Deliver me from any hold, guilt or condemnation the past might have on me. Please Lord; remove from my mind the person you removed from my life. Lord, instill in me forgiveness so that I can be set free. Lord, help me to search in the crevices of my soul so that I may not harbor any resentment, revenge, spite, cruelness or bitterness towards that person that hurt me the most and help me recognize that they were needed in my life. Lord, I ask you to renew my mind, restore my soul, bind up any wounds and transform me so I no longer live with regret about what used to be. Help me Lord to not think about the "could have, should have, and would have" help me to cast all those thoughts into the sea of forgetfulness. Thank you Lord for turning what the devil planned for evil in my life for good. I ask these things in your son Jesus' precious name. Amen.

POINTS ON THE PAST

It's the consequences of the thing that you did wrong, that will make you do the right thing.

Don't get over your past so much that you forget about it completely.

Studying and learning from the past makes for a better future.

Accept that yesterday is gone and what you have to look forward to is tomorrow

Let go of the things that have clouded your heart, for only a pure heart can see God.

Forget the things that are behind you and reach forth towards the things that are ahead of you.

Whatever is done, is done and over with.

What's ahead of you is so much greater than anything behind you.

God recycles our failures so we can use them in the future.

Nothing we go through is a waste or in vain.

Everything you go through is training for life.

Quit wasting time on thing that can't be changed.

God is a God of second chances, he holds nothing against you, so refuse to be trapped in the past, get past it and start living a new today.

Let go of the old so that you will have something new.

Once you realize what God can do in your Now, you will not want to go back to your Then.

2
Nothing Just Happens

*I*n your life, you will have good days and you will have some not so good days. Please keep in mind; the good days will in the end outweigh the bad, so really you should not complain. No matter what happens in your life, good things or bad things, know that nothing, absolutely nothing that happens just happens. Learn that whatever happens will happen for a reason and it will be easier for you to live through all the things that you will live. Many will be the seasons you experience during your life. There will be good seasons and there will be bad seasons, there will be the ones when you will be called to celebrate and get this, there will be the ones when you will be called to suffer. Yes you read it right, to suffer. No doubt about it, the enemy will send trouble your way, God though who is so merciful will use what the enemy sends your way to get your attention and to define your purpose. There will be times when you will be going through such tough stuff, that your life will seem like a total mess. I mean you will feel like you are all jacked up. There will be times when you feel like you have been, left alone and forsaken, well you are not alone, and you have not been forsaken. You will have times when you will want to die in fact a part of you does die. Just like Jesus did not die in vain, and rose again on the third day, so will you. Once you have risen you will able to witness about the things that happened in your life, and help others because, you will know that everything happens for a reason and "nothing just happens."

You are not Alone

Have you ever felt like you were alone? Like there was no one you could turn to, talk to? Oh come on, we have all been there at one time or another. Let's be real, something you went through or something someone did to you made you feel so down in the dumps and alone that you rather been dead. Right? I know I have been there; done that, have a t-shirt. I am here to tell you it is okay, even Jesus while he hung high and stretched wide on the cross felt like he had been left alone and asked God why he had forsaken him. If Jesus, who was perfect in all ways felt that way, imagine us who are no where near being perfect, of course we are going to feel alone in the midst of our suffering? I am reminded of some powerful words I once heard; those words were "Don't look at your situation, hold on to your revelation." Boy, I sure wished I had heard those words when I was going through that terrible time in my life. How sweet life would have been back then. I hope they are not too late for you, I hope they touch you and help you through whatever it is you might be going through at this moment. Most importantly whatever your situation know that you are not alone.

I'll take the Suffering

To be more like Jesus you, just like he did, you will have to pay a hefty price. Are you willing to pay whatever the price? Think about it, don't just say yes. Say yes only when you know that many times suffering to some degree is the price and you are willing to pay it. Understand that there is a purpose to suffering. You see, sometimes the only way the Lord can reach deep inside to necessary places that need to be reached inside your soul is through suffering. Through the suffering you endure you will grow and find salvation. The suffering that is caused by your hardships, your adversities, your relationships and your struggles will all shape and mold you into who you ultimately become. Believe me, one day you will be happy for all you've suffered. On that day you will thank God for everything because you will finally understand that there was a reason for all the things that happened to you, you will know that they didn't just happen.

> *My brothers and sisters, whenever you face trials of any kind, consider it*
> *Nothing but joy, because you know that the testing of your faith produces*
> *Endurance and let endurance have its full effect, so that you may be mature and complete, lacking in nothing.*
> *James 1:2-4*

God, who loved his son so much, didn't even spare his son from grave suffering. What would make you think he'd spare you? God knew that Jesus had to endure suffering, and carry our sin in order become complete, and offer salvation to the world. Just as it was necessary for Jesus, to endure suffering he did not want to go through. Sometimes it will be necessary for us to carry the cross and go through suffering we'd rather not and experience the agony Jesus did carrying his. I'm telling you like someone told me years back, "sometimes you have to carry the cross". Just as you allow yourself to feel the pleasures of life and celebrate them, you must also allow yourself to suffer for it is through our suffering that our character is built.

Can you not see that the Lord often makes himself known in our lives only through our hardships. I tell you if it wasn't for suffering some of us wouldn't know him right now, so take the suffering knowing that it's for something and know that whatever you go through, no matter the suffering, it does not negate what God has for you, in fact it is a necessary and crucial part of the plan.

But we also boast in our sufferings knowing that suffering produces enduring and enduring produces character and character produces hope and hope does not disappoint us.

Romans 5:3-4

The End Result

One thing for sure is that your God in heaven knows your whereabouts at all times. His eyes are never off you, so it's not like you'll slip on by him, he'll miss you and oh, oh, there you go, you miss out on his blessings. Oh no! He knows where you are at, every second. He knew you before you were conceived in your mother's womb. He knew your name before you were given a name. You were in his mind before you were ever in the past. He has had a plan for your life even before then, so if you think you were an accident, think again. Honey, no matter the circumstances surrounding your conception, weather you were a child conceived through rape or a one-night stand in the back of a pick-up truck. you were fearfully and wonderfully made, created with a plan in mind, you were no accident. Oh no you were planned by God, backwards planned I might add. That means he knew the end before the beginning and he created you knowing everything that would happen to you and all the choices you would make, the good, the bad and the ugly. To achieve the end he has planned for you, the Lord will orchestrate your life in such mysterious ways you're mind will be blown away. In the end though it will all come together and you will know why you were born. You will even get to say "For Such a Time as This"! Let me tell you something about God, he works in such a way that even the setbacks in your life he will setup for you to make a comeback. He'll make it so that the terrible things you go through will bring you closer to him and what he wants for you. Praise him and give him the glory he deserves for in the end, your life will be the result of everything you lived. Now, don't get me wrong, by no means saying these things determine who you are, they do however determine who you become. They do not determine where you are going only where you are at and where you choose to go. So thank God for all your battles, thank him for all your failures, for your betrayals and your heartbreaks for they have been training for whom you ultimately become. One day you will have to use what you learn, and it will come to past the reason why you were born and went through the things you did and learned the things you learned. In your life there will be those times when everything seems perfect, just the way you expected, after all you've been faithful, you have served, you have sowed so many seeds, you've done all the right things why wouldn't you get favor? Right? Wrong!! There will be times when everything is contrary to what you expect in return for the right person you have been and all the right things that you have done. Do you get my drift? I mean, here you are being a servant, being pure, good and holy and you are still going through some stuff. Honey, let me tell you something, sometimes, you will feel like Murphy's Law applies to you, because everything that could go wrong will go wrong. Excuse me but do you not know our enemy the devil? Isn't it just like him to make a mess of things when you are doing the right thing? Can you not tell what's really going on here? Girl, he's trying to get you to give up. Don't fear, the Lord has a reason for things going wrong. During the times when you have to endure struggle and face adversity, be positive by thinking that these things are tests of life you must past and that you are close to your promise land. These things if not handed over to the Lord are bound to make you feel discouraged. Don't let them, flow in what you know, or should know, the many, many promises the Lord has made to you. Make him your anchor and surrender everything to him. One thing is for sure you will have to take tests in life in spite of the fact that you are doing the right thing, at the right time for the right reason. The bible is filled with such examples. If you don't believe me read the story of Daniel and the Lion's Den. Now that's a perfect example of someone who was doing all the right things and still had to endure struggle and face adversity. It didn't matter, that he was doing it all right. Daniel still ended up in the wrong place. Like Daniel, you could be doing the right thing and still end up in a Lion's Den yourself, also like it was with Daniel it could be with you, a person you thought loved you and who you loved could be the person that sends you there. Regardless, of who does you wrong or what wrong things happen to you, remember nothing just happens and in the end it will be better than it was in the beginning.

In All Things, I Thank You

Thank God for all the things that come your way. I mean every single one of them—the good, the bad and the ugly. When you fail, don't get mad at him, for through it all he is perfecting you and getting you to where he wants you to be. Take it from me, had he not let you fail, you would have continued to do that wrong thing you were doing and you would not have been able to endure what you would have had to face had you continued. You know the things, the boyfriend who the Lord removed from your life, had he not removed him from your life, he would have ended up cheating on you, leaving you broken-hearted and devastated even more than you were, you know that position you thought you should have gotten promoted to but didn't, that forced you to seek a better opportunity, had you gotten promoted you would have remained with the company and then been laid off when the company closed it's doors. Learn and grow from everything that happens to you and remember it for remembering will remind you of how much you can take. Come through all these things stronger and better, not weaker and bitter. Understand that these things were necessary for you to appreciate your triumph.

> *For this slight momentary affliction is preparing us for eternal weight of glory beyond all measure, because we look not at what can be seen but at what cannot be seen; for what can be seen is temporary, but what cannot be seen is eternal.*
>
> *2 Corinthians 4:17-18*

I remember one day meeting this wonderful guy, I sat next to him on a flight. I tell you in the 2 hours it took us to fly from San Juan to Miami; I thought I had met my "dream guy". We started to get to know each other real quick, I mean we were on the phone hours every night, we lived a thousand miles apart so on the phone is how we got to know each other, what we wanted each other to know anyway. Things were moving so fast, we were talking about relocating and 17 days later he came to where I was at so that we could spend a weekend together. Everything seem perfect until, I told him I had children. You are probably wondering what took me so long, well my kids were away with their family during this whole time, it's not like they were there where he could hear them, see them or anything. Once I told him, he could not deal with it, he told me "wow you are so wonderful, you have everything I have been wanting in a woman, I have fallen in love with you, I just wish I had met you a long time ago, before you were married, before you had kids". I told him, "no you don't, I wasn't like this then, I am who I am because of all I have been through, because of all I have suffered, because I was married young, because I was divorced young, because I have been a single mother most of my life. Going through all that I have gone through has made me who I am, the woman you fell in love with, and if you can't accept that, than I'm sorry for you"! He obviously wasn't able to see it, but I did, I knew that there was a reason why I had lived what I had lived, and why so many things had happened to me. I started to appreciate it, and thanked God for it, in spite of my temporary pain (a month later and my "dream guy" and I were not talking much) for I knew that one day someone would love me because of all I had lived and would love my kids.

> *For everything there is a season, and a time for every matter under heaven:*
>> *a time to be born and a time to die;*
>> *a time to plant and a time to pluck up what is planted;*

a time to kill and a time to heal;
a time to break down and a time to build up;
a time to weep and a time to laugh;
a time to mourn and a time to dance;
a time to throw away stones and a time to gather stones together;
a time to embrace and a time to refrain from embracing;
a time to seek and a time to lose;
a time to keep and a time to throw away;
a time to tear and a time to sew;
a time to keep silence and a time to speak;
a time to love and a time to hate;
a time for war and a time for peace.

Ecclesiastes 3:1

Tests of Life

God is not the author of the evil that comes into our lives, however once it is there, he will observe how we handle it and will determine if we pass or fail at the experience. In other words, do we take the test again? It's amazing how the Lord has a way of orchestrating the things that the enemy puts into our lives to achieve his divine purpose by turning them all around for good. He has promised to work out all things for good, now that's a promise from someone who has a perfect track record of keeping his promises. I mean you can take it to the bank. What does this mean? It means that he never takes away from us without giving us back something better, in other words he gives us "double for our trouble"

And we know that in all things God works for the good of those who love him, who has been called according to his purpose.
Matthew 8:28

I have already established that things that happen to you will serve to shape you and to build your character, they will make you a witness, and will give you direction, get this-they were meant to be stumbling blocks but instead will become stepping stones into your future. Girlfriend, you know those barriers that were high and mighty above you and didn't let you get to your promise land, you will be able to tear them down and one-day walk across like a bridge to your destiny. Have no doubt about it. Now about these tests, let me tell you more about them, for you really need to know about them so that you can recognize them. All right, the first thing you need to know is that they will come in many, many forms. They will come in form of disappointment, disillusion, discouragement, betrayal, rejection, failure, and/or abandonment. I tell you life would be much easier once you accept the fact that these tests are unavoidable and needed in your life. Do not attempt to spend your days trying to protect yourself from them, if you do, you will one day make the sad realization that you have lived too scared to live your life and it has gone by. Now I am not telling you that adversity, struggles, tests, and all the things that happen because of them will be eliminated, oh no, by no means am I telling you that. The truth is that there is no way out of them, what I am telling you is that accepting the fact that you will have tests and you will get through them will minimize the negative experiences and make life while you are going through them more manageable, I mean if you know you have to go through something, wouldn't it make sense to just go through it and get it over with? Look at these challenges in life as tests you must pass to get promoted or to go to the next level. Think about it, final exams, SATs, bar exams they all come before a promotion right? If you fail in passing one, what happens? You have to take it again of course?

Well such is the same for these tests of life: adverse situations, struggles and every negative experience that could happen to you. What makes you think there is no promotion after you past tests of life? On the other hand if you fail, or refuse to take a test, you'll still need to learn the lesson. So guess what you'll have to take the test again.

God knows that if he made your life just roses, he would not be promoting your need for him therefore; He will throw in some thorns every now and then to prick you and hurt you so that you'll have to run to him for the pain to be healed. Just as a child runs to his or her mother or father when they are hurt, and trust their parents to kiss their booboo and make it all better, so does God make your booboo all better. When the thorns of life prick you, God's desire is for you to run into His loving arms so He can heal what's been hurt. There will be times in life when you think that the thing you are going through is going to kill you, I know. I know because I've been there and even wanted that. The pain I felt when my relationship ended, I thought was going to kill me. Guess what God said to me about that? He said, "I love you my child, kill you is not what I want to do to do to you, in fact what I a want to do is make you need me and help you find me". "I am wanting to give you the power that only comes from knowing me". HE let me know that if I looked to Him for strength and power, I would get through whatever I was going through, which by the way was no more than what I could handle, for He would not entrust in me something I could not live through". Does that not give you a sense of relief? Of peace? It should.

> *I have said this to you. so that in me you may have peace. In this world you face persecution. But take courage; I have conquered the world!*
> *John 16:33*

No Pain, No Gain

You've heard the saying, "No Pain, No Gain". Think of this one "Where there is Pain, I will compensate". I really feel that the Lord desires for us to know this. You need to know that the things that happen in your life, they don't just happen, everything, I mean absolutely everything that happens to you even the most painful things are significant and meaningful, they are vital and designed for the purpose of making you grow, making you into who God wants you to be, therefore they happen for a reason. Know what the Lord has planned for you and you will be okay, in spite of all you will go through.

> *For surely I know the plans I have for you, says the Lord, plans for Your welfare and not for harm, to give you a future and a hope.*
> *Jeremiah 29:11*

Praise God! There is gain from our pain. Isn't it good that things don't just happen and that you will be compensated for all you live through, knowing this fact, doesn't it make life just a little bit easier? All things bearable? So you see the mere fact that you don't see a purpose in whatever you are going through does not mean there is none. I am reminded of the story of Joseph in the bible. Think about it, all the adversity he went through, being sold into slavery by his own brothers, then being falsely accused for a crime he did not commit and sent to prison for it. It was many, many years before he finally got compensated for all he lived but he did and oh his reward was so good. Now about what you are going through, you could end up like Joseph suffering for many, many years. Think about it this way, it could be that you or someone you know will need that thing you learned soon, then again it could be 20 years from now, you might not even know it until then. It might be that the things you are going through right now, so you see those things that make no sense at all to you right now, will make sense some day. Like me, your ministry could be the result of the misery you have experienced you just don't know it yet, maybe that is why God allowed you to get passed, whatever it is you got passed. Believe me someone somewhere needs what you have gone through and you are going to be used to teach them. God will eventually use all your difficult times, oh yes, rest assured he will want you to use what you learned from the experiences you lived at one time or another. Keep in mind that when God directs your life, he doesn't see it like you, I mean we see just a scene, he sees more than that; he has the whole picture in plain view. When he does something he knows exactly what he is doing. So you see that heavy thing you are pulling the one you feel is draining you is in fact making you stronger. Now girlfriend, isn't it wonderful to know that you will go through nothing in vain? That through the pain there will be gain?

There will be times when you feel like you alone feel the way you do; you think that no one has ever gone through your hurt and pain. You might tell yourself something like "come on no one could survive this thing I'm going through" "no one could be hurting as much as I am" "no one knows what I am having to go through". How do you think I know what you're telling yourself? I know because I told myself the same exact things on more than one occasion. Honey, I've got news for you, you feeling sorry for yourself does you no good. It's time to stop having a pity party and thinking about yourself as if you were the only person there ever was. Pleeeease get out of that "victim" mentality, it is so unattractive. The truth of the matter is that people all around the world have gone through or are going through the same thing or something far more worst than what you are going through, the faster you realize that, the better off you will be. You are stronger than what you think you are, you don't know this but the Lord has already determined your weight limit and He will not; I say again He will not give you to bear anymore than you can bear. God will not allow for you to be tested past your limit, he would not let things happen to you if you could not handle them. Now isn't that good to know. No matter what you are going through, He is there with you and will Give you the strength you need to make it through. The bible says that if we use our faith, God will move on our behalf. He will make us strong. Know that the enemy roams about like a roaring lion, looking for weak people who have no faith and character; those who give up easily are the only ones he can devour. Those who are strong and do not give up and put up a fight he will ultimately end up giving up on. Remember this when things get tough and believe me they will, you cannot give in, you cannot cave in, and you cannot quit.

> *No testing has overtaken you that is not common to everyone. God is faithful And he will not let you be tested beyond your strength, but with the testing He will also provide the way out so that you will be able to endure it.*
> *1 Corinthians 10:13*

Life as a Garden

Now then, take a look at your life a little differently, than what you are use to. Are you ready? Okay! Let's look at your life as if it was a garden and you are its gardener. That's right look at your life as a garden. It's made up of fields of hopes and dreams, and all these wonderful things. Okay, let's back up first, its ground is fertile, broken with adversities, enriched by disappointments, fed by failures and watered with tears, plenty of tears. As the gardener, you will have to spend some time working the fields of your garden, planting seeds in the spring time and going through the summer, fall and winter sometimes without anything producing. The seeds you plant will be the things you learned from all you go through, I'm talking about adversity, betrayals, heartbreaks, failures, and so on. You will work the fields by watering them; you water them with your tears, the tears you cried through all those things that happened to you. That's right girlfriend, all those things that happened to you and made you cry, they were all needed to water your garden and help it to blossom. Imagine that? Okay another news flash for you: No one, absolutely no one can water your fields but you.

How sweet and simple it would be to learn from the things we see happening around us, from the misfortunes that happen to our friends, from our girlfriend's broken heart, without our heart ever being broken. Unfortunately it doesn't work like that—we have to go through these things ourselves. The good news though is that when we are done with the hurting and the tears, the fields in our garden will have been watered and we will begin to see our garden blossom beautifully, better than anything we had expected. I have seen a wonderful, beautiful garden blossom from my life. Just as it happened with my garden, your garden will blossom and surely you will reap a harvest. So do you get it? Really, really think about it, isn't your life just like a garden? Remember, only God can take everything that you have gone through, every test, rejection, neglect, disappointment, failure and mistake and cultivate reproduction out of them, by directing the tears that were caused by them to water the fields of your hopes and dreams.

Woe to the world because of stumbling blocks! Occasions for stumbling are bound to come, but woe to the one by whom the stumbling block comes.
Matthew 18:7

Final Word

How wonderful that everything that God allows to happen to us doesn't just happen. Rest assured with the peace that passes understanding that everything that has happened to you or will happen to you is for a reason. Take it from a girl who was raised in poverty, who's been abused, who's had her heart shattered, who was betrayed by her best friend, whose parents never told her they loved her. I have been through many struggles in my life, a great deal of adversity. I have suffered plenty and cried much, maybe more than you, maybe less than you. Whatever, I have suffered, but I have arrived at a point where I can see gain in my pain. I have arrived at a point where I am grateful for all that has happened in my life, absolutely every single thing for it has brought me closer to God and resulted in me being who I am today. When I think about my Lord, how He saved me, how He picked me up, how He turned me around, it makes me want to shout hallelujah, thank you Jesus, Lord for you alone are worthy. Thank you for all you have put me through, cause even if I can't see it, I know you have a purpose for everything you do, for with you "nothing just happens".

Prayer

Dear Father God, I come before you and thank you for everything that has happened in my life, I know I have had some bad days, but the good days outweigh the bad so I won't complain. Lord, I thank you because you are a promise keeper and have promised me that you will work out all things for good. Lord, I ask you to bless me in the midst of my trials and adversities. I thank you right now for them, for it is through them that I will become stronger, grow closer to you, glorify you and be prepared for what you have in stored for me. Lord, open supernatural doors in my life today, and give me double for all my troubles. Lord, I ask you to help me see with my spirit and not my physical senses, and help me take back everything that the enemy has stolen from me. Right now, in the name of Jesus, I cancel every plot, plan and scheme he may have devised against me and command him to flee in your precious son Jesus' name. I speak life and hope into every area of my life that seems like it is dead, or too hard for me to live. I ask you Lord to bless me in my spiritual, physical, emotional body, my relationships, my children, my home, my decisions, my career, my finances, my ministry, my leadership my future husband and everything that I do. I thank you Lord for you have a purpose for me and because you will not give me to bear more than I can bear in Jesus' mighty and precious name. Amen

3
No Is Not Always No

Okay ladies let's get real and get down to business. Now that we have already spent some time on struggles and adversity, let's talk about those 2 very important attributes that you must have in order to make it through all the things that will happen in our lives. I'm talking about faith and patience. There's no doubt about it, the greatest challenge you will face in your life when it comes to your faith and patience is during those times when you will have to carry the burden of disappointment. Times of disappointment are inevitable and sooner or later just like I did; you will have to endure them. Remember what you have already learned, that nothing just happens. Now don't feel bad, it's okay to feel the way you feel, you can love God, know his promises, and still want to give up, cave in and quit in the face of disappointment, it's a natural feeling. Even the most spiritual, faithful, patient person will doubt in God, his restoration, and his blessings after they have felt the burden of realizing something they hoped would happen, would not. This disappointment would cause anyone brokenness and despair. Without a doubt the greater your anticipation is for something to happen, the greater the disappointment when you realize you will not receive what you had anticipated. Ladies, it is especially important during the times of greatest disappointment, in your life, disappointment caused perhaps, from a failure, a broken covenant or betrayed trust, that you remain strong and steadfast in your faith and patience, so that God's will for your life can come to pass. Do not focus so much on what has gone wrong in your life or who has left it and try to make it right, or make them come back so bad that the rest of your life just passes you by, instead live your life focused on all the good and know that although God said no to something "no is not always no".

Through Faith

The bible depicts in Hebrews 11 many stories of people who remained strong in their faith and were patient. These people saw promises that came to pass because of their faith, and patience. The people in these stories did not let the circumstances that surrounded their lives keep them from the future that was God's will. There's the story of Noah who by faith built an ark to save his family from a flood, even when it hadn't rain, of David who by faith overcame Goliath the giant, of Moses who by faith freed the Isrealites from Pharoah, of the Isrealites who by faith passed the Red Sea as if on dry land, of Abraham who by faith became the father of many nations at his old age, and my favorite the story of the woman with the issue of blood who after 18 years she still had so much faith that she believed that if she could only touch the hem of Jesus' clothing she would be healed, she did and she was.

Although promises have been proven over and over again. Be advised, that during those times of adversity and struggles, when things will not turn out as you had expected, your faith and patience will be challenged. The enemy will send attacks your way to make you doubt and make you lose it, your faith and patience. However, when that happens you must be prepared to shield yourself from these attacks by using what he wants to use against you against him.

Hang In There

No matter the circumstances and how difficult they seem, whatever you are experiencing in your life at this moment, you must have faith and patience in God. He will see you through if you just hang in there. So how do you develop this faith and patience in God? Faith in God and patience comes from knowing him and his promises and trusting him. Now girlfriend, I realize that this is hard to do when you are faced with the loss of a loved one, when the man you have been faithful to walks out on you and your kids for another woman, when your "girl" has betrayed your trust by starting rumors about you, when you get no love from your kids, when you are waiting on a doctor to review test results and tell you whether or not you have cancer, when you realize that if you lose your job in the next round of layoffs you won't be able to make the next house payment. I by no means am suggesting you submit to self -denial on your issues, or that you ignore them, no not at all, what I want to get across here is this: just know that there is much more, know that whatever the circumstances you can survive if you have faith and patience in God. Just don't allow yourself to become so self-absorbed in what you went through or are going through that you lose sight of God's magnificence on your life. So what is this thing called faith? Let me tell you what it is. According to Webster, faith is the belief that does not rest on logical proof or material evidence. What else is faith? Faith is peace. Faith is doubting, your circumstances, it is being sure of things you hope for before you have them, faith creates expectations and gives God something to act upon and to respond to. God in his mercy will at times overlook our lack of faith and work miracles in our lives but for the most part what he responds to is faith.

Now faith is the assurance of things hoped for, the conviction of things not yet see.

Hebrew 11:1

Having faith that God will do what he has said he will do is very different than waiting for him to do it. Believing for what you hope for is hard enough in times of struggles, believing while you are waiting is harder yet. Nonetheless you must continue to have patience. Patience according to Webster's Dictionary is the capacity to endure a hardship, difficulty, or inconvenience without complaint. It means calmness, self-control and the willingness or ability to tolerate delay. It is when you exercise faith during the waiting period" and you are patient that God is pleased the most and will reward you for your faithfulness. We must remember that God can bless us in many areas of our lives at different times. He works in mysterious ways. Because of that we cannot overlook or minimize anything that is going on in your life. He could be blessing an area of your life while you are in a waiting period in another area. God's will and timing sometimes will not coincide with our plans, in fact most of the time they will not, however if you have faith and patience you will be able to do things his way and in his timing and see how things turn out better than you had planned.

Hope deferred makes the heart sick, but a longing fulfilled is a tree of life.
                                                                Proverbs 13:12

Disappointment & Brokenness

I told you we were going to get real, so let me share. It is through my own personal experience from many devastating disappointments that I share. I know what it feels like in your heart and in your stomach, when you want something so bad and you realize you can't have it. For me it was when I finally for the last time I realized that there was no turning back or going forward with the man in my life. Now I know that sounds funny, but so it was, I realized it many times, but then finally, there was the last time. When I realized it was over, the feeling I felt was one of devastation and complete brokenness. You know the kind, the kind that makes you feel like your nerves are shot, you can't sleep, you can't even eat, you feel sick, you feel like you have fallen and there's just no way for you can to get back up. No matter what is going on that's good in your life you can't seem to grab anything around you to hold on to. Regardless of how together you have it going on, you have to have faith and patience, or you have nothing. I tell you faith and patience, you will not be able to deal with disappointment and brokenness and you will become bitter. When you are bitter, bitterness will undoubtedly carry over to other areas of your life and you will begin to feel like everything around you is falling apart. Take it from me, I know, been there and done that.

Have you ever had to go through the type of disappointment or brokenness in your life that had you thinking that you couldn't survive? Have you ever doubted God because of your circumstances? Has the enemy tried to kill God's destiny for you? It's during these times in your life that you are most vulnerable. You cannot allow yourself to become weak or the enemy will come. He will come to kill, steal and destroy. I am here to tell you that you cannot allow him to use your disappointment and brokenness and the bitterness that results from it to bring you down. You must not let him steal, kill or destroy your faith and patience, if you do you are, through. You must lift your head up high and walk in victory, let what you are going through make you a better person for you don't know it yet, but, God has a future for you. The enemy knows that and will try to use things to make you think otherwise. Do not give him any leverage, whatsoever. Do not allow him to use this time to deceive you. Praise God no matter what the circumstances, if what you are going through is a work from the enemy and you have a good attitude he will see that his efforts to destroy you are futile and will become discouraged, he will have no choice but to leave you alone. Have you ever known anyone who wants to fight someone who is all smiles? Of course not, just like no one would fight someone who is happy and all smiles, and will walk away so will the enemy walk away from you if he thinks he is fighting a losing battle. If you have faith and patience you will stand firm on God's word and know that what the enemy means to bring you evil, God will turn around for your good. You will know this if you have faith and are patient. Now, get real, how many times have evil things happen in your life that you later came to realize had to happen in order for you to have the blessings that you now enjoy? I guarantee you that if you put your life in the hands of God, even the biggest, most painful disappointment can become something you will one day be able to thank him for. I know this for a fact for it was during the most disappointing time in my life that I discovered how truly blessed I was.

We know that all things work together for good, for those who love GOD, who are called according to his purpose.
Romans 8:28

There seems to be no words of consolation to relieve us from the feelings we feel during the trying times of our lives. So I won't try to tell you any. What I will tell you is that "this too shall pass" these words were of great comfort to me and have helped me tremendously during my times of disappointment. Do yourself a favor and realize that your life will be made up of not just one event but a lifetime of events. Events will be like company that comes knocking on our door, some you will invite in with hesitance, some you will welcome with open arms and some you will want to send away, what you have to realize is that you will have a lifetime of events, wherever you are at in your life right now, whatever is happening in your life that is breaking your spirit is just that-an event. Just like the company that comes knocking at your door, they just come for a visit they can't stay forever, neither will the event you are experiencing in your life, remember it is just one of a lifetime full of them, it can't stay forever.

For this slight momentary affliction is preparing us for an eternal weight of Glory beyond all measure.
2 Corinthians 4:17

There will be many other types of disappointments besides the ones I have already mentioned, to me however the greatest of all the disappointments you will face in life, the most tragic of all will be when you invest valuable time and fervent prayer in a relationship you believed in and hoped for with all your heart and not see come to "and they lived happily ever after" ending. There is nothing more regrettable than to realize you have no return on the investment you have made with your most valuable asset--your time -a precious commodity that escapes you never to be retrieved again. This disappointment is of an even greater magnitude when the person you believed in and hoped for did not even appreciate you, worse yet never even really knew the real you and ends up giving up hope and walking out on you when the going gets tough, totally abandoning all efforts that were previously made in the relationship and never even acknowledges the change you made.

To come to terms with the fact that you could have exhausted precious time and effort in more worthwhile things like God, yourself, your family, your friends is a very sad thing. It is especially sad when you lived your life in name of the person who has moved on and has left you stuck in a time warp wondering why he is not looking at the wonderful woman God has made you to be. When I made this realization I was totally devastated, I had spent seven years of what should have been the best years of my life and of my daughter's life on a man and a relationship that all of a sudden were, viola! Forever gone. Seven years of my life had escaped me never to come back again. I was left with my 2 teenage daughters I felt estranged from because for all that time in my life, I had made someone else who was no longer around a priority I had lived my life and achieved the successes in it mostly to prove things to him. I had changed to become what he wanted me to become and he didn't even stick around to see it. That time in my life was the most disappointing time ever, I could have very well lost it, my faith and my patience, remember the shot nerves, I couldn't eat, couldn't sleep thing. Praise God in the midst of it, instead of choosing to become bitter, I chose to become better. The word says that all you have to have is faith the size of a mustard seed and you can move mountains. That's all it takes. After all God had given to me and done for me, I could surely have that little bit of faith. I tell you having faith gave me peace about my circumstances. It made me realize that all the pain and hurt was not going to be in vain. God would not give me more to bear than I could bear and that things would be turned around in my life for his glory.

> *He said to them, "because of your little faith. For truly I tell you that if you have faith the size of a mustard seed, you will say to this mountain "Move from here to there and it will move; and nothing will be impossible for you.*
> *Matthew 17:20*

GOD's Many Answers

I am sure that by now you know God will always answer prayer. Now do you know that he will answer in many, many ways? Of the many ways that God answers prayers, one of the ways he will answer is to just say no. He will say no because he knows better. What we need to understand is that when God says no we need to accept his no, it might help you to realize that when he says no to some things he is saying yes to others, same holds truth when he says yes to some things he is saying no to others.

I really saw this revelation when I was compelled to see something positive when things were not going as I had expected in my life with the man I was with. The man I was with could no longer father children. God had put in my heart the desire to once again be a mother. If

God had said yes to that relationship that I wanted so bad, he would have said no to me being able to be a mother again, however by saying no, he made me available for a man in the future who could still have children, by doing so he said yes to the possibility of me becoming a mother again.

There are times in our lives when God answers our prayers just like we ask him to and then when he does we cannot accept it. There are times when God will say yes just because he sees that we want something so much, while all along knowing that no is the better answer, I tell you sometimes we have to be careful what we wish for, what we pray for and what we want. There were many times in my life when he answered my prayer exactly the way that I had prayed for, however I could not accept his answer, I prayed and pleaded with him many, many times for him to change his answer from a no to a yes, and many, many times he did. He granted the desire of my heart and gave me just what I asked him for, and boy did I pay for it over and over again to the point I wished he never had.

Before my heart was completely broken to pieces, I prayed to God that if the man I was with, the one I was hurting so much for was not the man he wanted for me for him to remove him from my life. He did just that, but I could not accept it at that time, I pleaded with him until he turned his no into a yes. I did not have the faith, or the patience to wait on God. I should have known that he would work things out. I should not have tried to take things into my own hands, by doing so, I made a mess, had I trusted and waited on him the pain, hurt and disappointment I would have saved myself from. God had spoken many times to me about this man many times before. He revealed to my heart that he was not who he had planned for me. God had begun to do a great work in me; he knew that I wanted to live for him passionately.

I began to thirst and hunger for him. I was seeking his word and guidance in everything that I was doing, I was serving, and I was faithful with my tithe. I had become pure and righteous. I was a virtuous, godly woman. I was even becoming forgiving and patient, these were two qualities that I had lacked in the past. The man in my life had not taken his relationship with God as seriously, he knew the word however he was not living the word, he was not serving, he was not tithing, he was wrestling with the flesh and fighting a spiritual battle. He was stuck in the past and living with unforgiveness, and resentment. God knew that if I remained in this relationship this man would hinder my spiritual growth and separate me from him. God removed him from my life, first from my home, then from my church, he brought his estranged children and his mother to live with him, therefore he would be busy working on those relationships and have no time for me also so that I could see how he treated them and realize that that wasn't what I wanted in a man. It took me a while but I finally learned and accepted the fact that the purpose of prayer was not to conform, God to our will but for us to adjust to God's will. I tell you I wish I had accepted his no when he first gave me his answer. I did not and because of it I could see God looking down on me and saying, "Girl, you just had to go on and have it your way, you just couldn't let me handle it, well I let you have it your way and look what happened, if only you had listen to me, if only you would have had faith and patience in me, how different things could have been".

God's word says that if we walk in righteousness he will not withhold anything that is good from us. Therefore if it has been withheld it was not good for you. God gave us his son, what makes you think he would hold back anything else from you? As a mother I know that if I offered my daughters to anyone for anything, there would be nothing else I would hold back from them. I mean I wouldn't tell someone "you could have my daughters but not my dress, not my shoes, not my car. You can't have that. Of course not, if I give someone what I love the most, why wouldn't I give them everything else I had. Why would I keep anything from them? Could you imagine God telling you that "girl, I gave you Jesus, but you can't have that job, you can't have that raise, you can't have that house" etc. of course not. God wants to give you so much if he gave you his son, he won't stop at anything else. Girlfriend, understand our God is a giving God. Even when he shuts a door, he will be sure to open another door. Don't be like so many women who stay looking for so long, so hard and regretfully at the door that has closed that they fail to recognize when he has graciously opened another door for them to walk through. Remember that if God takes something away from you he is gracious enough to replace it.

If God has said no, rest assured there's a reason. Could it be that he can see into the future and see that if he says yes, it doesn't look good? Remember He alone can see your yesterday, today and tomorrow at the same time in one glance, therefore he knows that what you want today could hinder what he wants for you tomorrow. God loves you too much to not take away from you something that will hurt you. If it's going to hurt you he will not hesitate to use tough love on you and firmly tell you no. He is willing to see us disappointed today if he knows that we will be able to enjoy our tomorrow. Could it be that he is saving his yes for something that is far greater, sweeter, and richer for you? Girlfriend you need to know beyond the shadow of a doubt that God has a plan for you. You will see it at the proper time, and you will thank him for it if you just have faith and be patient.

Sometimes we are confused and wonder how God is working things out, we can't seem to understand his method of operation, I am here to tell you that it doesn't matter if you can't understand how he works, what matters is that you understand that he does operate and go with the flow. Trust in him and let him do what he needs to do, let him make you become the woman he wants you to become.

Not No, Just Not Now

There is something that you need to know, that is that God's no doesn't always mean no, it could simply mean not now. In other words he is not denying your request, he is just delaying it. I spent many years in sales management and training, I trained my sales people that no doesn't always mean no. I would tell them a no today could be a yes tomorrow. No could really mean different things. It could mean that right now is not the right time; it could mean that there are other things that are more important at the present time. I would tell my team, accept the no and move on; every no brings you closer to a yes. I think that is exactly what GOD is telling us sometimes when he tells us no. He is saying, "right now is not the right time", he is saying, "There are other things that are more important right now". Maybe he feels that what you are asking for at the moment is not something you are ready to receive. It could be that he still needs to work on you and prepare you for what he has planned for you. This is especially true when it comes to the matter of bringing someone to you. Satan will deceive us into losing faith and patience. His goal is to drive us to just settle for anyone. I tell you sometimes no one is better than just anyone. It is in this area more than any other that you must have faith and be patient. God does have a plan for our lives that plan includes someone for you to spend your life with, however if he deems it necessary he will withhold that someone from you and not send him your way until you are absolutely ready to receive him. Could it be that he is waiting because he is still working and preparing the divine man he has for you? You never know he might not be quite healed, and needs to do some forgiving before God brings him to you. Maybe it is you he's working with, there might be a need for healing or submission or forgiveness that needs to take place in you before you are presented to him. Consequently you will have to wait until you are both ready for you to meet. I remember when I accepted this truth, I use to kid around and say "Boy, my future husband must really have some issues, because God sure has been working on him for a while". In the meantime remember that the Lord is a Master Potter you are merely clay, on his wheel; you need to let him mold you and shape you into his masterpiece. Trust me if you get off the wheel before it is time, before he is done, you will make a mess of your life. Let him do as his promise says let him complete that good work he has begun. Remember that his thoughts are not your thoughts nor are your ways his way, his thoughts and his ways are higher than yours.

> *For my thoughts are not your thoughts, Nor are your ways my way, says the LORD. For as the heavens are higher than the earth, So are my ways higher than your ways and my thoughts than your thoughts.*
> *Isaiah 55:8-9*

The Reason for the Season

There is always a reason for the season, regardless of what season you are in in your life, spring, summer, fall or winter put all your trust in him, God will not make you wait anymore than you have to, only as long as you have to, true he doesn't conform to our standard of timing but he is always on time, he is never late with his promises. God's timing is perfect. Don't lose hope before you know it he will present you with a perfectly timed gift. Sometimes he will come when you least expect him, but he will come, he will come when you put your trust in him, he will come when you thirst and hunger for his word, he will come when you have shared intimacy with him, he will come when you tithe, he will come when you serve, he will come when you seek him first.

God wants for you to have life and have it abundantly. He is your protector and will not fail you. You have entrusted your eternity to him, why would you not trust him with your future? It is safe to put your life in his hands. It is safe to trust him. Remember there is nothing that is too hard for God. There is nothing that is too hard for you if you have him in your life, with him all things are possible. He is so faithful there is not one need you could have that he has not addressed with a promise.

I can do all things through him who strengthens Me.
Philippians 4:13

In Sunday School one morning my Pastor, Earl McClellan used an analogy that really opened my eyes to this, it went something like this: Remember when you were a little kid and you heard the ice cream truck coming down the street? You wanted ice cream so bad that you went running down the street to get some, you wanted the ice cream so bad that you didn't even look to see if any cars were coming when you crossed the street. Then God just grabs you and whisk you away out of harm's way and into safety just as a car was speeding by. When you get up you realize that the ice cream truck was turning around and coming down your street so you hadn't missed it, you were going to get what you wanted you just had to wait. You see God knew that if you just had patience you would have gotten what you wanted without getting hurt. Boy, this really had me thinking and I felt that the LORD had placed it in my heart to share something on it when Pastor was done. I did. I took it just a bit further and related it to my impatience. I shared that there were times when I wanted ice cream so bad, that I couldn't wait till the truck came down my street, I wanted it then, so I went for it, God was trying to hold me back from being hit by a car, and I just shoved him off. God finally let me go and I was hit by a car, I was not killed, I survived but I was crippled, and the ice cream, well lets just say it wasn't even worth it anymore. Had I just waited I didn't have to go through all that to get it. This is the God you have watching over you. Girl if he says no, you need to thank him, praise him and worship him, for there is an awesome reason why he is doing what he is doing, you just don't know it yet. However hard it is what you are going through at the time, no matter how much it hurts be grateful for it, hurt has it's rewards. I assure you he has saved you from something that could have been much, much greater.

If you are in total resistance of God's plan and timing for your life, he will not force you to conform to his plan. Neither will he force you to wait. He will give you the choice to do things your way; my question to you is why would you want to? Think of the times you have, don't you wish you had waited? In many of his promises God has warned us to wait, to not grow weary, he has promised us that if we do the right thing, in due time we will reap a harvest, one that is of reward. God has told us to be careful, to trust in him and that he will work out all things for good if we believe. He loves us so much and desires for us to listen to his sweet soft voice and obey him until the time is just right for him to pour unto us the blessings he has saved up for our lives. Do not wait to get to heaven to find out about all the blessings that were meant for you that GOD did not have a chance to pour out on you because you had little faith and patience so you decided to do things your way. I tell you it is up to you to take these words to heart and to live by them.

Be still before the LORD and wait patiently for him
Psalms 37:7

Father Knows Best

God is our father, and father always knows best. There are many women who have fallen victim to the enemy's deception, they have lost their faith and grown impatient, they have become weary and have compromised, by settling for something less than God's best for their will. The consequences are tragic for the women who choose not to develop patience and wait on God's will. The consequences include feelings of failure, heartbreak, loneliness, separation, divorce, and financial hardships, children that are left insecure as the result of their parent's unhealthy marriage, dysfunctional families and generational curses. The anguish that these women face is very, very sad. I assure you God never intended for his daughters to live such a life.

On the other hand there have been many women, Godly woman who have remained faithful and patient in the midst of the enemy's deception. These women waited on God's plan for their lives, they waited and they won. These women possess peace, joy, true love, security, healthy families, confident children and a future that is full of hope and happiness.

The next time you are faced with carrying the burden of a disappointment, when you feel you have no faith are running out of patience and don't feel like God is going to be faithful proclaim the following words: "God I don't know why this is happening, I don't know what you want my testimony to be, but I know you have a purpose and a reason so I will have one. Lord, I will trust in you and surrender myself completely to you. I give you all the thanks and praise knowing that you know exactly why you are doing what you are doing and one day I'll know the reason. God work in my life so that you can receive the glory and so that your will not my will be done."

We must learn to be thankful and accepting of answered Prayers, in fact we need to praise God for them. Remember God always answers when you pray, it's just that sometimes because the answer is not what we wanted it to be we seem to think our prayers are unanswered. Be thankful for the times you thought your request was denied for it might just have been delayed, be thankful of closed doors for when God closes a door, he is sure to open one too, be thankful even for rejection for you might not realize it but through it you find direction. Praise God and be thankful for one day you will understand why your prayer wasn't answered the way you wanted it to be or why it was delayed and see all the blessings in disguise he sent your way.

There are some prayers God cannot answer until you respond to the ways he is dealing with you. He will not give you all his blessings until he can have all of you, you must be obedient in all area of your life. Our society has produced many successful people who are blessed with their skills and talents, with their finances, however they are missing something, while they are blessed in some areas of their lives, they are not blessed in other areas and have made this apparent. There have been many

Hollywood stars who seem to be successful who have committed themselves to rehab centers, who have been arrested, who abuse alcohol, who have become addicted to anti-depressants, who have overdosed on drugs, who have shoplifted, who have been divorced, who have been unfaithful. Could it be that they need to turn their whole lives over to God. It is only when you are obedient to God in all areas that he will command blessings over your whole life. You are obedient by your faith, by your patience.

> *GOD is not a human being, that he should lie, or a mortal, that he should change his mind. Has he promised, and he will not do it? Has He spoken, and will he not fulfill it?*
> *Numbers 23:19*

If you are struggling being faithful and having patience commit yourself right now to trust God with everything in your life. Commit yourself to wait for his best. He is truly able and faithful to do what he has said he will do. You can be sure beyond a shadow of a doubt of what you hope for and cannot see. I challenge you no matter what is going on, when you don't know what to do, there is always something you can do, praise and worship him. You may even want to pray something like the prayer at the end of this chapter.

Put Some Action to It

James said, "Faith without Works is Dead". That is so true. Whatever you are experiencing; whatever you want to experience you must give God something to work with so that he can make things happen. Faith alone cannot be relied on. Only when you put action together with your faith will you see things begin to happen in your life. Sometimes you have to get out of the boat like Peter did. He had Faith in the Lord, yet he didn't wait on him to come to him on the water, instead he got out of the boat and began to walk towards him, all the while staying focused on him. The same holds true for you; you will never find your destiny by just praying. So what do you do? You pray, you go to church, you get a prayer partner, you praise God, you give your tithe, you forgive, you repent, you let go of fear, and you renew your mind.

Think about it, buying a house, finding a job, getting a Degree, fixing your credit, having great mannered kids, saving your marriage. Tell me is any of it just going to happen by praying and having faith? Of course it's not you are going to have to find a house, look for a job, study for exams, pay your bills on time, discipline your kids, trust your husband.

There is something about faith that makes you act, it will make you forgive anything, it will make you serve, it will make you give, it will make you press forward. Faith without action is really not faith. Do the best with what you have and give God something to work with. With God you don't need much, he could multiply the smallest thing, just give him something.

Have Faith, Be Patient

Be prepared for there will be struggles you will have to endure in order to get to the point where you surrender all to God and allow for his will to be done in you life. Faith and patience can change everything, and can be used as a shield to offer you protection they can have a positive impact on anything you are facing even the worst of circumstances.

Know this struggles and tough times are unavoidable and they will come, they'll come because we create them, they'll come because the enemy wants to deceive us into thinking we cannot trust in God, they will even come because they are the only way God can take us from where we are to where he wants us to be so that we can depend on him and give him the glory. It is then that he will pour unto us his blessings. Rest assured struggles and tough times will come, but they won't stay long. You will fall down, but you will get up. Before you know it the tough times will be gone. Have faith, be patient.

Final Word

In this chapter I shared about the 2 important attributes you must possess and that are essential for you to make it through life and all the things that are going to happen. There is no doubt about it, faith and patience are not easy to come by, however are attainable by knowing God and his promises, and trusting him. Among many things, I covered in these pages, were disappointment and brokenness, I even went into sharing about my own broken heart which I found as a release to do, which by the way was wonderful to do. I really hope that I was able to teach you about God's many answers, especially that his no isn't always no and that sometimes what he really means when he says no is not now. Most importantly what I hope you learned from reading this chapter that "no is not always not".

Prayer

Heavenly Father, I come before you and ask you to help me to submit to your ways. I ask you to strengthen my faith and to give me patience. With all my heart, I want to believe in you, your word, your faithfulness, your promises, your ways, your timing and your power. I admit that I have tried to take matters into my own hands and have done things my way in my timing and because of that I have felt empty, hurt and dissatisfied with my life. I confess that I have been afraid to trust in you totally. Right now Lord, I surrender to you, and release you to do what you want to do, I lay down my life and all my ways and ask you to take control of it and make me the person you created me to be. I commit myself to trust in you completely. You have proven yourself to be dependable, trustworthy, and faithful and above all a promise keeper. Lord starting today I will look at you for my future and not my circumstances. Lord, I thank you for all you have done and all you will do in my life. Lord, I ask you to speak to my heart and reveal to me the road that I should take, and remind me always that you will never leave me or forsake me in Jesus Name. Amen.

4
Forget the Sex

*I*t is almost tragic to see how our society has reduced making love, which should be a beautiful thing to a mere act called sex. In reality, making love and sex are by no means even close to being the same thing. Advertising and marketing campaigns everywhere these days use sex to sell anything and everything. You see sex in commercials, in advertising and in billboards. You see sex in regards to cigarettes, jeans, cars, beer and many more consumable items. The entertainment industry uses sex to promote their music, magazines, videos and movies. There is no doubt about it, the enemy has a field day dressing up sex to make it look inviting, then he grabs a hold of you with it and makes you feel like trash. The devil makes sex look like something that brings only pleasure and no pain. After all, you always see a smile on someone's face or hear a joyous sound from someone who's been involved in it, right? You never see tears or pain associated with sex, do you? In reality sex, I am talking about plain old sex, the type that happens between two people that are not married and at times don't even know each other, will bring pleasure, oh yes it will. Yes it will make you smile, and sound off, but even more so than that, it will bring tears and pain to match the pleasure. So learn what it is to love and make love and "forget the sex".

And the Difference is?

The difference between making love and having sex is drastic however; this fact is never accurately portrayed on television or on big screen. It is sad how the consequences of just plain old sex are never brought to light. It leaves us with a misconception of what sex really is. Sex the act, is something that is very easy to do. It is so easy that people are doing it at a younger age each year. Sex, as it is so often portrayed in the media, is simply about finding relief. It is something that fulfills the needs of the body and it alone. Sex in that context is over in minutes. With much endurance, stamina and these days pills it can last hours. Making love, the way it was intended to be, now that is hard to do. It is something that is done by mature adults and not until they are married. Making love is about fulfilling the needs of the heart not just the body. In this context, this act can lasts a very long time not just minutes or hours. Making love is different than sex in that it is an ongoing process. It is something that evolves over time.

Easy come, easy go, slam, bang, thank you mam, affairs will not last. They are like boiling water in a pot, once it evaporates it is gone because there is no substance at all to it. Sex is just that something without substance. Sex seeks to fulfill the outer-self, the body while making love seeks to fulfill the inner-self, the heart. Making love involves much more than the tangling of bodies and the exchange of bodily fluids. It involves trust, caring, communication, friendship, admiration and respect.

These are things that last a lifetime these are the things that allow for making love to be possible. These are the things that will make your husband think twice when lust enters his mind, and the devil shoots the fiery dart of sex at him. These are the things he thinks about when it crosses his mind what could happen with the beautiful confident looking woman who just walked by and didn't give him the time of day so he wants to prove he still has it or when a pretty young thing who uses her sex appeal to come on to him. The ability to make love is the result of all these elements, the trust, caring, communication, friendship, admiration and respect coming together and leading to commitment and marriage. It is in this context that GOD ordained for sex to take place and to give us pleasure. It is in this context that you will achieve the maximum fulfillment this act can bring. The participation in this act outside of the marriage covenant is just a counterfeit that the enemy waves in our face again and again. I assure you it will bring you as much pain as it does pleasure.

There is no better sex than sex when it is done as a means of communication, and expression of love in marriage rather than just a release between two people having a fling. Sex is only really great, I am talking about in a spiritual sense here not a physical sense when you do it with someone who you have come to know and allow to, know you. This someone could only be your husband. Believe me you will want to forget every other man, no matter how good he was, how great he made you feel. No woman wants to be touched and held by a man who does not take time to know her at all. By that I mean to really, really, know her. Okay I am sure someone is wondering "How do I know we will be sexually compatible, if I don't check him out first". Don't be shy believe me when I tell you I thought the exact same thing. I mean, I had been out there, and I knew what good was, I wanted some of that, at least I thought I did. If the man you are with is sent to you by God, your lovemaking will be wonderful, true love has a way of making things that way. What? Do you not think God is interested in your sex life? He wants you to enjoy each other. If that doesn't give you any comfort than think like I did, "what about that great sex you have had, where did that lead you? How did you feel once it was over?

No testing has overtaken you that is not common to everyone. God Is faithful and he will not let you be tested beyond your strength, but with the testing he will also provide the way out so that you be may be able to endure it.

1Corinthians 10:13

I tell you it is easy to feel erotic, passionate, intense feelings, the one that runs like blood through your veins, the one that makes you melt and makes you tremble. I have had the wild sex which does that to you. I'm talking about the kind that has you half-naked before you can make it up the stairs to the bedroom, the one that has you on the kitchen floor before all the groceries are put away, the one that makes you pull over on the side of a road. This type of passion is exciting for sure but not lasting. This type of passion can in fact deceive us by blinding us to the point we don't realize that we are in trouble until it is too late. Sex puts us in danger of destroying our emotional and spiritual health, and forces us to endure heartbreak that will linger on long after the sex is over. Take if from me girlfriend, those moments of ecstasy I don't care how good they are; don't make up for a lifetime of pain. The hurt that you feel from it can be so strong that it can completely make you forget about how good the sex was.

Ties that Bind

By the age of 18, I had already been involved in 2 sexual relationships both guys had not only touched my body, they had touched my emotions and entered my heart. Both of these guys broke my heart and made me feel used. They made me feel a way I never wanted to feel again. To protect myself against further heart I remember telling myself that the next guy I had feelings for I would marry". That's exactly what happened. I met my husband when I was 18, just 8 months after my first heartbreak. He was an older man, ten years older, unlike the other guys who were my age. Of course, I thought that as an older man, he had his life together. Our relationship started out physically. We had what with my limited experience I thought was great sex. He asked me to marry him right away, I said yes. Never mind the trying to get to know each other. After a while the sex was just that, even though I had never had much more I knew that there had to be more. It's like there was something missing, when he started abusing me physically, I could no longer give myself to him. When the sex stopped, we realize that there was nothing else holding us together and the marriage ended. After that I was pretty much out there. I really couldn't tell you why, I don't remember feeling empty so it's not like I sought to fill a void I felt through sex. In spite of being hurt, I never thought I set out to hurt guys. I absolutely loved sex and knew that I could use my sex appeal to get any man so I did. I was no wh____ and never did I have a one night stand, but I did have many partners, most of which were my friends. I remember looking at it as us doing each other favors. Some men in my life very few I called "boyfriends", that meant we were exclusively with each other that is until, I became scared of the relationship and ended it. Some men in my life were sexual partners or what the guys refer to as "booty calls". I called them when I needed them. No man thought of me "being out there" even after being together we would never even talk about it again. It's like I had a secret life when it came to sex, I didn't share it with anyone, only my closest friends—two or three of them knew about the guys I was with. When I think on it now, it's like GOD was with me even then, he protected me, it was he who gave me the wisdom to use protection so I never became pregnant from a man other than my husband. I never caught a disease, nor was I raped when I decided in midstream that I wanted to stop. Many, many years went by before I fell in love and settled down with one man, the man I thought would be it, the one that ended up breaking my heart. I was 28 when I for the first time really, really fell in love. I thought I had been in love many times before but never with someone I could see myself spending my life with. The man I fell in love with was one of the guys who had broken my heart when I was 18. We had remain friends for many, many years and it just so happened that after 10 years we found ourselves at the same place. Immediately after we met I tell you from the first night we were sexually involved and started an intense relationship that lasted for many, many years. Our relationship was filled with passion, lust, excitement and lots and lots of sex. Our relationship was also filled with hurt, pain, infidelity, mistrust, and emotional abuse.   At first, we were so excited about the fact that we found each other after so many years and our sex was so good and exciting, it blinded us to obvious issues and challenges we should have been able to recognize from the beginning. For almost a year we spent just weekends together mostly in the bedroom, having marathons, if you know what I mean. We wanted to learn how to please each other so much we didn't expose ourselves to the everyday things of a relationship.

We didn't work on learning how to please each other when it came to matters of the heart, in other words matters that took place outside of the bedroom where you spend most of your time. You see that's what happens when you introduce sex and passion to a relationship. It is difficult for a man to stop wanting sex and just be satisfied with getting to know you and your heart, or developing a friendship. As far as he is concerned, after he has become acquainted with your body and has been satisfied by it and knows that he can satisfy you, there's not much else he needs to know.

Therefore a man leaves his father and his mother and clings to his wife, and they become one flesh. And the man and his wife were both naked, and were not ashamed.

Genesis 2:24-25

I always knew about GOD but it wasn't until a couple of years into my relationship with this man that Jesus was introduced into my life, then a little while longer until he started working on me. I remember one Sunday morning listening to my pastor preach a sermon on Sexual Intimacy, and how sex was suppose to be in the context of marriage. Wow it blew me away. I was by myself in church that morning and I remember crying throughout the whole sermon, I realized then that something very crucial was missing in my life. I realized that it was in fact true what I had long since thought, that there was much more to sex. I realized then, that I had lived my life putting so much emphasis on sex. It was soon thereafter, that I started changing I was convicted of what I was doing. I decided that I no longer wanted to have sex, not until I was married and I could make love.

And those who belong to Christ Jesus have crucified the flesh with It's passions and desires.

Galatians 5:24

69

Imagine telling your lover, after years of passionate, intense, wild, great sex that you no longer want to have any of that. Imagine telling him that you want to wait till you're married for him to make love to your mind, body, heart and soul. It didn't go very well. I mean that was the part of our lives that was great, it was the part that was holding us together, he loved it and now I was going to deprive him of it. Right then he proposed and of course I told him we were not ready to get married because of all the issues we still needed to resolve, issues with communication, trust, honesty, finances. Not only that, I didn't want to rush into marriage just so that we could have sex. My lover loved me, he also loved GOD but not to the point where he was convicted about this issue, therefore he refused to surrender his flesh. He would always say that that was his weakness. He would want to have sex even while he knew, I lay crying about the guilt I felt doing what I knew was wrong. Well it so happened that after a while I not only no longer wanted to have sex, it was something that hurt me both physically and emotionally.

> *For this is the will of God, your sanctification; that you abstain from fornication.*
> *1 Thessalonians 4:3*

I was in this relationship for a total of 7 years, it was so intense that for almost 2 years after we had officially ended it we were still emotionally involved and somewhat physically involved. Keep in mind that I had long since committed to the fact that I no longer wanted to be in sin and refrained from the total sexual act, however we satisfied ourselves in other ways, ways that I finally came to realize were not part of God's will and needed to be reserved for my husband and for his wife. I was very challenged during this time; the struggle with my flesh was at times overwhelming. There were the late night phone calls from "him", the surprise visits, the waking up to lustful dreams in the middle of the night, memories playing over and over in my mind, of the things we used to do, there were so many things that triggered something that made me remember our life together especially that part of it. Then of course there were the feelings he made me feel. I loved the fact that he wanted me so much even after so much time had gone by. I loved it when he told me I was the only one. I loved it when we would see each other and he would kiss me out of control and hold me tight while he told me "I miss you, I love you, you drive me crazy, the way you make me feel no other woman could ever make me feel, you're the best, I desire only you. To know that I had that power over him was very exciting, it really drove me crazy. I realized after some time though that it was not what I wanted to have. I knew that I was on very dangerous ground and that it was going to be hard to get out of, but if I was to live for GOD, I had to let go. This thing that held me bound for so long was soul ties. You see when you have sex with a man, and give him your body you also, give him your Soul.

The Cutting of Cords

It is very painful to break up with someone who you have had sex with, as oppose to someone you have not had sex with. The word says "the two shall become one", therefore God created sex to be a bond that binds 2 people together like a seal. When you try to break from this relationship the soul is torn, and that will hurt.

Beloved, I urge you as aliens and exiles to abstain from the desires of the flesh that wage war against the soul.
1 Peter 2:11

Although there had been many other guys in my life this had been the first time that I had given myself totally and completely to a man, I mean my heart, my body and my soul. I found myself having the greatest sex I had ever had not because of what I felt physically but because of what I felt inside of me. I was bonded so strongly physically and emotionally with this individual that when the relationship ended, the hurt I felt from it was devastating, it was like something that was unbearable. I realized then that it is harder to break-up with and get over a man if you have not had sex with him, could it be because sex was created by God to seal a couple together in marriage? I tell you once sex is present a soul tie that is not easily broken is created. Remember, the word says "the two shall become one" and that is exactly what happens when you have sex. That is why when such a relationship is broken your soul is torn. That's exactly how I felt torn, and it hurt if you know what I mean. Had it not been for God's word that says he will not give us to bear anymore than what we can bear, I really don't know what would have happened to me, I remember at one point even thinking that people could really die from a broken heart for I felt pain in my heart that was excruciating. You are probably wondering why the relationship ended? Well let me just say that he was not the man God had for me or it wouldn't have ended. In spite of all the love it just wasn't enough, I think it had lots to do with the fact that we didn't come to know the Lord till much later in our lives and in our relationship. We didn't know much about having renewed minds, and restored hearts. We didn't know about forgiveness and that with God all things are possible. The sex in the beginning definitely did not help. I guess you can say we sowed some bad seed and those seeds had to be reaped.

For many, many months after my break-up, I pretended to be this girl who was tough, and who was over it. I acted happy after all, there were so many wonderful things going on in my life. In reality I was really feeling lonely, like a part of me had been destroyed, more like it had died. I felt like a failure, I was always so successful, always got what I wanted. Here was the one thing that I wanted more than anything and I just couldn't get it right. I couldn't share what I was experiencing with anyone. I could get no consolation from my friends whatsoever, on the contrary the things I heard about my breakup were things like "that's good", "that's the best thing that could have happened" "you could do so much better" "girl that man is not worth your tears, you could do so much better". For a very long time I just kept things locked inside all of it the hurt, the lost, and the disillusion. I finally decided I could do much better and I did, I dedicated my life completely to God I renewed my relationship with him and once again declared him as my Lord and Savior and started living for him with passion. I realized GOD was the lover of my soul not any other man and that all I needed was him. I accepted that old things had passed and that I was made new and started to feel restoration.

I met a wonderful man, who was very godly, he had fallen in love with me and my daughters, I mean, he had fallen in love with me as a person, not my looks, not my sex appeal, not my nice body, not how I could satisfy him for he didn't even know, he had fallen in love with who I was, with my heart. He saw me as a beautiful woman because of who I was and not what I had. As much as I tried to see this person as someone GOD could have sent for me, I couldn't. I couldn't because I still had ties with "him", the man that had been in my life. When a good friend asked me why can't you see yourself with him? I responded, "I want magic, I want the magic I had with "him" I want to see him and want him like crazy" I said. My friend responded, "do you realize that you are wanting what you had before and in doing so, you are going to get it--all of it, what you want and what you don't want. This statement really opened my eyes to see things differently, I realized that I was still bound by my strong sexual desires and I needed to be set free. I realized that if I wasn't set free, I could be blinded by passion and could be mislead. I realized that that "magic" I was wanting could be an obstacle to me recognizing true love. After all I had read so many stories about people who ended up in love totally to people that they were not initially attracted to. I even knew people this had happened to. What I finally realized was that I had been doing something wrong by having ties with "him" and that GOD wanted me to do what was right. I knew that I had to do the right thing; it was the only way that GOD would bless me with a man that would love me and that I would love back. I remember dropping to my knees in tears and asking God to deliver me and erase from my memory that memories that I had. It was after this deliverance that my life changed.

Good Lover vs. Bad Lover

With all that being stated, let me tell you in more detail what both a good lover and a bad lover can do to us. So what makes a lover a good lover? An unforgettable lover? What does he do? Let me tell you what he does— when he kisses your lips, you feel softness in your in your heart when he touches your body, he reaches down even deeper to grab a hold of your soul. When his eyes look into yours they speak to you without him having to say a word. Who can forget that kind of lover? A good lover ensures their lover is pleased, not just himself. He desires to give pleasure knowing that in giving he will receive. Now that's what I am talking about. He will want to make your time together special he will want to meet your every desire he wants to wine and dine you, he will want to romance you, he will want to make love to you not just in the bedroom but outside its door. This is the type of lover that will hold you tightly during the night long after the act is over. The one that you will wake up to and catch looking at you while you were sleeping as if you were Sleeping Beauty, This is the type of lover you want to hold on to forever and never let go. Girl, we ladies need this kind of lover, a lover who is a lover of the day as well as the night, he needs to be the lover of your soul and everything that is within you, not just your body.

Let me tell you now about a bad lover, what does he do? This type of lover can also be unforgettable but for other reasons. He seeks to satisfy only his needs, when he does seek to satisfy your needs he does it with the intent to feed his ego which is still being selfish. A bad lover is all about the hips and the lips forget about making the experience special, he will not care about the romance, excitement, gentleness, sweetness and holding you through the night, forget that, when this guy is done he will turn his back to you. This lover will be right next to you and you will still feel alone. Girlfriend, understand that a good lover is someone you can count on when the going gets tough. A good lover is not a man like most women think one that can perform acrobatic feats in bed and who has a body like "Rocky". Who cares if your lover has a body and can move his hips if he can't help you stand up when you fall, if he can't protect you from the storms of life.

Do not be rushing to have a lover, GOD will bring him to you when you are ready. You must first renounce anyone you have had sexual relations with. Cast them out of you life forever or they will hold you bound. They will be a hindrance to you having pure thoughts, and make you think about you having sex instead of allowing you to think about making love. You need to know, that until the man you will marry and make love to comes into your life, you have a lifetime lover, his name is GOD he, will please you and fulfill you like no other man can. He will never leave you or forsake you. You also need to know that if you don't feel that he can meet your needs you will be challenged for the one that he will send you will not be able to meet them either. After all it is God who is more than ready to have a deep lasting relationship with you. If you can't practice a relationship with him that is free from the fear of rejection how could you practice and have one with your future husband?

> *I know that nothing good lives in me, that Is, in my sinful nature. For I have the desire To do what is good, but I cannot carry it out. For what I do is not the good I want to do; no, The evil I do not want to do--this I keep on Doing. Now if I do what I do not want to do, It is no longer I who do it, but it is sin living In me that does it. So I find this law at work: When I want to do good, evil is right there with Me.*
>
> Romans 7:18-21

Ladies, you need to understand me when I tell you that there are many things you should not do to or for just any man, on the other hand for sure there are many things you need to do to and for your husband. Please read this carefully and heed to it. By no means use your sex appeal to get a man, if you do that is all you will ever have, I know what I am talking about. Now once you are married, use that sex appeal, drive your husband wild, romance him, in the privacy of your own home, excite him in ways that he never thought imaginable, be creative, and daring, surprise him every now and then and check this out, don't ever, ever, ever deny him pleasure. When you marry loose yourself completely to our husband, have an affair with him, if you don't, there will be someone there who will be ready to have one. Be on a mission to make his every fantasy come true. Do not pretend to make the marriage bed a place of structure and boredom, the marriage bed should be a place where you and your husband become engulfed in erotic and exciting play, it should be about fulfillment, the kind that last more than mere minutes or hours at best, it must last a lifetime.

The Enemy's Tactics

You need to understand that the enemy's most commonly used weapon against us is sexual sin. He knows that sexual sin is easy bait and can have a devastating impact on our lives. He is well aware of the fact that it will separate us from GOD more than any other sin and will not hesitate to use it if we allow him to. He has a way of setting us up to feel down and dressing sex up to look so good that we give into it. Think about it. He will make us feel unloved, unwanted, lonely, rejected, and vulnerable until we mess up, when we do, we will then have to pay up. Believe me it's not worth it, the price we pay to feel good. In the end what felt so good, doesn't feel so good and worst feelings will we have to face.

Sin is lurking at the door; its desire is for you, but you can master it.
Genesis 4:7

The enemy has used this tactic against us throughout all the ages of the time. There are many examples in the bible that witness to what sexual sin can do to our lives, in particular there's the story of David and Bethsheba in 2 Samuel 11.

As with any other sin, there is restitution for sexual sin. The consequences for this sin are grave, at times even tragic, as in the above mentioned story there can be even murder. Other consequences are diseases, unwanted pregnancy which result in abortions, adoptions and single parenting, there's infertility, there's adultery, low self-esteem, low self-worth, there's lost of character, dignity, honor, integrity, careers, not to mention the scars of shame and regret that sometimes last a lifetime. Our society has witnessed many prominent men who have suffered grave consequences after becoming victims of this sin. There's Bill Clinton, Jim Baker, Gary Hart, Jesse Jackson, Marv Alberts and Jimmy Swaggart. Although I have no women to mention here, rest assure that many, many women have suffered because of their sexual sin, it's just that our suffering is a lot more personal therefore at many times silent. We don't usually lose our careers and wealth, but their dignity, self-respect and self-worth none the less are lost.

You are probably wondering if I suffered consequences for my sexual sin. Believe me I did, very much so, I didn't experience them until much later in my life. I was completely honest about my sin with the man I fell in love with, he knew everything, there was to know about me, I mean everything. He knew so much he could not deal with it. He never allowed for my sexual sin in the past to stay in the past. He would always bring it up even at the moment of our own intimacy. It was literally like other men joined us while we made love. He would remind me of this sin constantly especially when he wanted to hurt me. Because of our sexual sin, neither one of us was ever able to trust the other nor did he never really respect me. He became more obsessed with me than in love with me. I know that because of what he knew about me he never really wanted me as a wife, but still could not let me go when our relationship was over even after he had met a woman he wanted to make his wife. The baggage of our sexual sin was too much for us, and especially hard to carry once I told him I no longer wanted to be physical. Ultimately our sexual sin became a major contributing factor to the end of our relationship and destruction in our lives.

It is my sincere belief that what you sow as a single person you will reap as a married person. In other words the more sexual sin you have committed in the past, the more baggage you are dragging around and will bring into your marriage. This is baggage you bring to bed with you every time you share intimacy and make love with your husband. That's why they say that when you sleep with someone you sleep with everyone they have ever slept with. It's true. Imagine that. When you to go to bed with your husband you are also in bed with all the men you have ever been with. What's even more disheartening is that you take GOD with you as well. If that is not enough to make you stop, I don't know what is.

For the ways of man are before the eyes of The Lord, and he ponders all his paths.
Proverbs 5:21

I remember after the September 11th tragedy, the emails and stories that were floating around, I remember one picture in particular it was of an eagle with the reflection of the World Trade Center in his eyes, and a tear drop falling. If you looked at that picture, you could tell the eagle was in pain, he was really hurting. Picture God, that's what he does when he sees us in this sin. He cries. He's in pain, he's hurting. Why does this sin hurt God? Unlike most sin, sexual sin is ultimately sin against yourself and will hurt you, it's when you have committed sexual sin that you do not trust, it's sexual sin that makes you doubt your self-worth, it's sexual sin that makes you commit adultery easily, when things aren't working out, it's sexual sin that makes you think your husband is being unfaithful, it's partaking in sexual sin that makes you hurt when things don't work out, it's sexual sin that keeps you bonded to that man you know is no good for you and want to let go of.

What a Man Wants

Girlfriend, don't let a guy fool you, guys will keep quiet about it and not let you know, they might make us think they want a "wild thing" a woman of experience, if you know what I mean, but they really love it when they have found a woman who is keeping herself pure. A woman living in purity these days is a rare find, one that is very valuable. A man values this kind of woman, because she will be interesting, and a complete mystery. Oh and how it boosts a man's ego to think he could have something no one has been able to have, her heart is something he will want. Not to mention how it will excite his imagination. Now when you have given a man everything including you have including your body too soon, you have done away with interest, you are no longer a mystery, and your value decreases. I experienced this first hand when I learned my value decrease significantly, after the guy I had given myself to completely, left me for a woman he had found who had been living in purity. Let me tell you this is not a good feeling, take heed for my wish for you is that it's something that you never have to live through. So you see if you want a man, don't let him know about all your experiences, what you did with who and surely don't show him what you can do. Let his own imagination take him where you will not, and keep him interested in what he could have. Attract a man with your purity and Godliness; let him see your passion for the Lord and the Holy Spirit working in your life and you will keep him around for good.

So what if it doesn't happen quite like this? What do you do? I'll tell you what you do not do, you do not compromise for less then what God has for you, do this and the man you've met will be drawn to God, his determination to win your affection once he has realized what a rare find you are will drive him to it.

A Virgin Again

As I am writing this chapter, I can tell you that this is the place where I am at in my life right now; I am a virgin and proud of it. I am staying holy and pure. I have been this way for years now. If someone had told me I would go years without sex, I'd think they were trippin. Today, I am waiting for the man GOD has for me. So what, that my gift has been unwrapped over and over again, my sins have been forgiven and washed away, I have been made new, I have decided to rewrap myself, stay pure and save myself for the man who will be my husband, my lifetime lover. I once read that GOD celebrates pure sex within marriage and when a husband and wife revel in it, it becomes a jubilant two person worship service. Imagine that. Wow! I think of that when I think of my honeymoon night. I look forward to it with much excitement, I am storing my passion, and have great anticipation for a pure desire that will make everything new and fresh, it will be the best sex I have ever had because my husband will make love to me the way no man has done, he will make love to my heart, mind, body and soul. You know what your friends in the world say "try before you buy" that won't matter because with GOD satisfaction is guaranteed.

If you are in a relationship, think about what it is based on, is it sex or is it making love? If it's sex, no matter how good it is take it from me, it's not going to be that good forever, so save yourself, put a stop to it right now wait and get a real love life, wait until your honeymoon night to make love. You will be glad you did. Don't give to someone something they have not earned or deserve. Don't perform a role you have not yet been given that of a wife, for it is she who should give herself to her husband not the girlfriend. If you are just starting a relationship and have not crossed the line of physical intimacy, stop while you are ahead and save yourself from irreparable damage that doing it will cause, don't think about introducing sex into it and don't even talk about it. That old cliché' that "The way to a man's heart is through his body" is a lie from the pit of hell. Sex was designed by God to express love not to be the foundation for it. It is something that comes after a commitment is established and a covenant is made. So what if you know this is going to be the man you marry? You probably think its safe right? Not. I tell you if the man really loves you, girlfriend, if he really does, he can wait. You are probably thinking by now "come on now, you don't understand", "you don't know when was the last time", "You must not know how it feels" Oh believe me I know, I have been there, and as far as how long its been, you have no idea how long it could be until you try it. Take it from me when I tell you if you try walking that tight rope of temptation you will fall. I assure you waiting to make love will be much better if you wait. Enjoy fulfillment that last more than a temporary moment, enjoy fulfillment that lasts a lifetime. Waiting on that someone that will be your husband to make love with will be worth the wait.

Shun fornification! Every sin that a person commits is outside The body; but the fornicator against the body itself.

1 Corinthians 6:18-20

As a lady you need a lover who is a lover of your day as well as your night. He needs to be the lover of your soul and everything that is within you, not just your body. It is important for a woman to know that she is desired as a woman not an object. I tell you it will not be enough that he caresses you and strokes your body until you is satisfied. That is temporary, what you seek is permanent satisfaction. You need a lover that will care for your mind, your spirit, your heart and your soul. Lady when you have a lover, that's a lover of your soul, your eyes will sparkle, your smile will be bright, your voice will have softness and compassion, your movements will be with security.

The Real Honeymoon

There is no doubt about it, sex is absolutely wonderful, It is a thought and sensation that could linger in your mind forever, it provides a high like nothing else you can experience, the pleasure it creates and the way it makes you feel can not compare to any other action you partake in. It is an overwhelming feeling that makes you feel both breathless and alive at the same time. This all makes it very hard to live without it once you have had a sample of it; it's quite obvious that a desire that makes you feel so alive and good would be something that is hard to stop. However, in spite of all those exhilarating feelings, if not done at the right time, with love and in the context of marriage as it was intended to be done, it can and will become something that is wrong. Girlfriend let me tell you something, if you are in it because of lust, you'll never be satisfied. Lust never satisfies completely. It will always leave one wanting more. It is something that becomes shameful and that GOD condemns; something that you will one day regret. However making love the way that God intended for it to be done, will be something, that when it happens, will make you feel totally complete. Wait until your honeymoon night, kneel before your Lord God and let your husband unwrap his gift. Do not let your honeymoon be "business as usual" let it be a real honeymoon, the night of your life.

Final Note

No doubt about it, we got into some serious stuff in this chapter. I am very glad we did, we had to, I mean that's was one of my major reason for writing this book, I wanted to address issues people are unwilling to address that need to be. I don't care about how a man's brain work and how many times a day he thinks about sex, we women think about it too, and sometimes simply need to shed some good light on it. Alright enough of that, I really hope that of all the good, important stuff we covered, I hope you have a better understanding of the difference between sex and making love, and that there is no better sex then the sex with your husband. Remember that once you have been with a man that's not your husband you will have ties that bind you and not easily be broken, but can be broken. You can be a virgin, no matter how wild you were, you won't even miss it. Forget about the good sex you've had, wait on the man God has for you and honey, I promise you, you will experience the greatest sex you've ever had and afterwards you'll be glad you stood firm and said "Forget the Sex".

Prayer

Heavenly Father, I willingly submit my flesh to you as a living sacrifice. Lord, I ask that your spirit will guide me in my walk towards purity and holiness. Help me Lord to honor myself and to value my body as you value it, let me be a rare find for the man you have for me, let him be attracted to me because of my purity and godliness. Lord, help me resist the enemy's tactics and my fleshly longings so that I do not sin against my body and against you. Lord, I ask you to give me strength to cast out any memories of my sinning against the flesh that I will never think about those times, and forever cast them into the sea of forgetfulness. Help me Lord to completely break any ties that I at one time formed because of it. Lord, I ask you to instill in my heart, my mind, and in my soul the vision of how you want me to come together in a union that glorifies you and to share my love in intimacy with the one you have chosen for me in Jesus' name. Amen.

Sayings on Sex

Sex will never result in love.

Sex outside of marriage is 100% physical and 0% spiritual.

If offering our body for sex is all we have to offer, boy are we in deep trouble.

Sex was created by God and distorted by Satan.

Oral sex, phone sex, it's all sex.

When it comes to sex, if you don't want to get burned, stay away from the flames.

Sex is a nothing but a release.

If you demonstrate self-control with sex with the person you are with trust will follow.

You form a soul-tie with everyone you have sex with. Those ties once broken will make you feel like your soul has been torn off.

Sex alone no matter how good it is will not be good forever if that's all it is. It will not make you happy beyond the minutes it last.

Forget about people and what they say about having to try on before you buy. Not to worry if God has his hand in it you will have satisfaction guaranteed.

Save ALL things in regards to sex for the one God has for you.

How great it must be to not have anyone in your bed but the one that will be married to you.

Breaking up with someone you have had sex with is far more painful than someone with whom you have not..

5
Single and Satisfied

Every woman has a longing in her heart to find true love. In this regard, we each need a Cinderella story of our own. There is absolutely nothing wrong with wanting to be married. Believe me when I tell you, your wanting a husband is okay. Every woman wants to be a wife and have her own husband to come home to, to talk to, to hold on to, and, of course to make love to. Sadly, in this world of matchmaking, dating, weddings, and having babies, women sometimes struggle with being single and rush into getting married. Sadly, single women fail to see the wonderful opportunity they have before them as a single. Instead they become anxious in wanting a husband. In reality, it can be such a wonderful thing to be single. If you are single, know that you are in this season for a reason. Accept it and learn to live your life to the fullest right in the midst of where you are. It would be tragic for you to think you have to wait until you are married to do so. Take pleasure in being single! When God sees you are ready, he will bring you the man he has for you. I myself have been there where many single women are. I have been anxious and have thought a lot about being married. I realized there was nothing I could do, but wait for love to find me. Until then, I had to be the best single woman I could be, fall in love with my Lord and work on myself while I wait. Today, I can honestly say that I am by myself, content and truly happy. I say of myself I am "Single and Satisfied!" Stay with me… I will share with you things I discovered that helped me to get there, and you too will proclaim I'm "Single and Satisfied!"

A Void Filled

Back to wanting a husband. I have already said it, its okay, and in fact it is a perfectly healthy and understandable desire. It is when that desire becomes the focus of your life, if you think about it around the clock or when it makes you anxious, also when it affects every decision you make or don't make, that the desire of wanting a husband becomes wrong, and you my dear sister, are in a world of trouble. Can't you see that when you replace your relationship with God with the thoughts of a relationship with a man you don't even have yet; what you are really feeling is that God is not enough! How dare you think that! Believe me you could not be more wrong. God can fill that void you think you need filled by a man. You must realize once and for all, that you do not need a husband or a marriage to feel happiness or to have a full and complete life. You can be Single and Satisfied if you really wanted to be. It's very important for you to know that every moment you waste waiting on a husband for your life to begin is a valuable moment that you could be spending with God. During this time you should be preparing yourself for when your husband, the one God has for you, does arrive. That's right, so use your time wisely, maximize on every moment you have. Spend time building a stronger relationship with God and allow Him to prepare you to be a rich and valuable addition to your husband. Learn and practice to give and receive love in the present with people God has already placed in your life. Do not be so blinded by the desire to marry that you can't be happy during your single season and you convince yourself something is missing when it really is not. Better yet, do not marry just to marry.

I always knew that I had been created to share life with someone. I longed for that for a very long time, yet that person I was going to share it with was taking a long time to arrive. I started to grow weary, anxious and became frustrated. I wanted to be married so badly, the idea consumed me. Finally, I accepted that I needed to be happy and content on my own, while I was single. In doing so God would prepare me to be married, and one day make my husband a very happy man. I embraced the thought of becoming a better 'me', before I became a 'we' by making my Lord my husband. What a difference that made in my life. Never again will I feel like there was a void that needed to be filled. I became "Single and Satisfied!"

Happy in the Here and Now

For 15 years, I had been divorced. Only eight of those 15 years was I not single. I have been single for a long time huh? Girlfriend let me share with you some of the things I have learned through the years as a single woman. I have learned to become completely happy in the here and now. First, I decided to cultivate a love affair with the Lord, my God until my husband arrived. Experiencing intimacy with God and having a relationship with him is greater than anything you could experience with any man on earth; take it from me; I've tried it already. Through my experiences I have learned valuable lessons about living and waiting. Please pay close attention to the things I have learned. If you allow me to use my experience to help you, I believe you will find that you can be a successful and satisfied single while seeking the kingdom of God and his righteousness and live excited and happy until you are married. Surprisingly, you will be a better woman because of it and have a greater gift to offer your husband. You do want to be a gift right? Of course you do. It took me a while, but I learned that rather than become consumed with and resent my season of being single, I had to value this time that God had given me as a treasure. I tell you don't waste any time, you'll regret it if you do. Do not think about the things you do not have, a husband and children and lack of time due to distractions and responsibilities that come with them. Instead, think about what you do have, time...lots of it. Okay so if you are a single mother, I can feel you. Maybe you do not have a lot of time, think about it as a single mother you just have kids. When you get married, yes, you will have a husband that will help you with the kids, but then you will have kids and a husband. You will have to take care of your husband, your kids, a house and all that comes with it such as sex and a hot meal in between it all. As a single woman you have time to develop a real sense of spiritual, emotional, physical, economical and personal health that you will not have as a married woman.

> *Let each of you lead the life that the Lord has assigned, to which God called you.*
> *1 Corinthians 7:17*

The key to enjoying life in your present season is to know when God wants for you to be married, he will orchestrate your life in such a way that you will not have to worry. In case you didn't know, lack of joy is derived from wanting life your way and not trusting that God has you where he wants you. Let me tell you something, if you can't have life your way while you are single, you surely can't have it your way when you are married. Believe me life can be satisfying whatever your season, if you have God in it and let him be in control. Do not waste valuable years waiting to get married for your life to begin. Do not wait until it is too late to realize that the time you lost was valuable.

> *Not that I speak in respect of want; for I have learned in whatsoever state I am in to be content.*
> *Philippians 4:11*

My dear friend, do you ever feel as if God has forgotten about you? Are you getting tired of waiting? Contrary to what you think or feel, God is thinking of you every second of the day, and although you don't understand, He knows what He is doing. I'll tell you what you need to be doing with the time you have. You need to be getting busy about your father's business. You need to be getting a life. Recognize and accept the fact that having a man will not make you any more a whole woman than the woman you are now while you are single.

Many women have turned to someone seeking in them and from them what they ultimately must find in themselves through God. We will get more into this in a later chapter. I remember talking to my best friend on the phone months after my relationship came to an end. This friend knew there had always been a "man." She asked me if I was ready to have another man in my life and I told her I had decided to stay single and to be happy by myself. I wanted to wait before another man came into my life and I married. At this time my friend had been married for about twelve years, she revealed to me something I had not known before. She told me that six months into her marriage, she had complained to her husband that he wasn't making her happy and she expected to feel happy when she became married. She told me that her husband replied, "If you married me to feel happy then you made a big mistake. You need to be happy yourself, because you aren't going to feel that from me!" How many of you know that, as cold as that sounded it was the plain truth?

It is a very important fact that a woman's solid relationship with herself is essential for the success of every other relationship she will encounter in her life. It is impossible to find a man who will appreciate you if you do not know and love yourself and communicate that to him. Others will learn to treat you the way you train them to treat you, you train them by how you treat yourself. Do not fool yourself into thinking that others do not observe you, believe me they do. They observe the things that you do and do not do. Your likes and dislikes, your strife, your class, and everything about you. A woman who is not happy with herself will seek recklessly to find happiness in others. This woman will be doomed. Her search will be futile and bring destruction to future relationships in her life. Not only will she continue to be unhappy, but she will also make others around her unhappy in her quest. This woman will in most cases love too quickly the wrong man, be hurt and then grieve for years. The bottom line is that if you are dissatisfied and unhappy, as a single woman, you will also be dissatisfied and unhappy as a married woman, so get busy at being happy.

My Father's Business

The perfect opportunity to spend time with God is when you are single. Think about it. If you have no time to build a relationship with Him, how will you have time for another? This should be your time to get closer to him and learn more about Him. You will come to love what he loves and hate what he hates, more importantly to serve Him and allow for his will to be done in your life. Don't try to rush this time, for there is so much for you to do. There are scriptures to be learned, unsaved souls to be won, His word to be spread, and a virtuous woman for you to become. Do all this while you have a chance and before time escapes you. My dear friend, you will lose something very valuable on your wedding day. You will lose control over what you do with your time. Why not use this time before your trip to the alter to focus on God, and serve Him. It's something you will not always have, and regret not having taken advantage of once you are married.

And the unmarried woman and the virgin are anxious about the affairs of the Lord.
1 Corinthians 7:34

Sadly enough, so many times we let our anxiousness of wanting to be married rob us of our precious time and the beautiful life God wants for us to experience while we are single. Be all you can be right now, don't wait until after you are married. If you do, you will find yourself uttering the words "If only I coulda, woulda, shoulda." Have your husband find you in the Father's house without having to search very far. That's right. Let him catch you working and being busy about your Father's business. You will be so excited and focused on what you are doing that you can't see anything outside of that, your husband however will be watching you. He will be so intrigued by what he observes, and find you so attractive because of it, that he will come to you.

He said to them, "Why were you searching for me? Did you not know that I must be in my Father's house?"
Luke 2:49

Don't you know that God ordains seasons in our lives, and will put you in a position where you will be most effective for Him? I know because that's what he did for me. Being in a season of singleness is one of those positions. When He decides that you will be more effective to Him married, believe me, He will position you for marriage in a way that you will be blown away. Accept the position because seasons of our lives cannot be prayed away. You will have to experience them so you might as well make the best of them. You need to know that our God is a God of order; there is logic to everything He does. Everything He does, he does with a purpose. His order and logic goes back to the beginning of creation. In the beginning, God created Adam and he was alone. His first and deepest relationship was with God and himself. It was not until after Adam's relationship was established with God that he said it was not good for man to be alone and he created Eve.

But strive first for the kingdom of God, and his righteousness, and all these things will be given to you as well.
Matthew 6:33

Even the strongest, most independent woman wants to have a husband she will feel complemented by and share her life with. Here I was living in sin with a "boyfriend" for years, even though I loved him, I couldn't see us getting married. We had taken a pre-engagement class in which I learned I was ready to get married but he wasn't the man I should marry. I think it was when I realized that, our issues escalated, and we went our separate ways. It was after the end of our relationship that I desired to be married. I knew that the next man in my life would be assigned by God to be my husband.

Here I was in my mid 30s, I was pretty, intelligent, and successful. I was the proud mother of two beautiful, extremely intelligent, gifted, Godly daughters. Both were very much involved in church, had good morals and could take care of themselves. I had an excellent job that I loved and was making more money than I ever thought I would. I had just bought and completely furnished a beautiful, custom built home that some couples couldn't even afford together.   I had, money saved, money invested, college funds in place, and was taking vacations out of the country every year, and all of this I had done on my own without a husband. I knew I didn't need a husband, I just wanted one. I wondered at times if there was something wrong with me; after all I had it together. "For sure I had everything a man would want," I thought.   Many men had come around, but none were the one. I remember once telling my friend about a man I had known for years. I had just talked to him; he was this great guy, and a Godly one at that…well he went to church anyway. I told my girlfriend some sweet things he had just told me I told her, "he's such a gentleman, he's never been married, he has no kids, he has a career, and he says all the right things, boy, if I let him, he'd make me his queen." "But"?….She responded, "He's not the king."   This friend knew me pretty well, she knew what I wanted and that I wasn't going to settle. Most of my friends and family had begun to think that I was picky and I'd never get married. I wondered what exactly it was God wanted to do with me; I had been unmarried for such a long time, and I was ready. In addition to being successful, I had God in my life. I was very involved with my church single's ministry. I led, served, and tithed faithfully.   I had great Christian friends and was leading single women's book study. All this and I still felt there was a void that I yearned to fill.   A void I thought nothing around me could fill. Not my beautiful daughters, my beautiful home, my job, my wonderful friends, not the guys that I was meeting and definitely not the money I had. I came to a realization deep down inside, the realization that not even a husband was going to fill the void I felt. I came to the realization that only God himself could fill the whole that was inside. Wow what a great realization that was, it was life changing!

In the Meantime

It was when I came to this realization and sought God passionately with all my heart and surrendered to being a happy single woman that my whole life began to change. So drastic was the change that I began to feel that being single was a blessing. I decided that I would no longer think of a husband, instead, I decided to accept God's will for my life, which was for me to be single. I decided that He would be my everything. I asked Him to reveal to me what His purpose for me was as a single woman, and He did. He revealed to me that He wanted to use me in my single life, to share my testimony and to serve other women. He wanted to make a message out of my mess and to turn my misery into a ministry. God wanted me to do this my writing this book. You see He could not use me effectively to write this book had I been married, had I not experienced the heart-breaking ending of the relationship that made me single. Once I started writing He even revealed to me that until I was done with his purpose for my life, he would not bring my husband to me.

> *The human mind may devise many plans, but it is the purpose of the Lord that will be established.*
> *Proverbs 19:21*

Talk about some serious writing, home girl got on it. In the meantime though, I enjoyed life. I loved being single. Seriously, I actually got to a point where I saw my singleness as a blessing. I became engulfed in His word and with doing His work. I knew that when the time was just right, and I was done with what He wanted me to do; He would send me the man He had been preparing me all along to receive, and to receive me. The anxiousness I once felt completely lifted from me and I felt calmness and peace like never before.

When I think back on my life, I know God was always there, he had been trying to do something wonderful in my life for a long time, and I just wouldn't let him. God's purpose for my life for the longest time was for me to be single. The funny thing about the enemy is that he knows what awesome plans God has for us and tries to mess them up. The first time I became single, when I really knew it was over, and God revealed his purpose to me I still was not ready to let go of the man that had left my life. I was still praying for us, hoping for a future and trusting God to change him. I guess you can say the enemy grabbed a hold of that and he used it against me. You see, he did not want to see God's will fulfill in my life. He knew I had an incredible destiny planned for my life. He knew my destiny would be a result of how I endured a devastating breakup and lived my life during my singleness. He could not afford for me to be single and see God's promise for my life come to pass. He set it up so that I thought there was a chance for a future with the man I loved so much. He figured that by my thinking this way, I would be distracted and kept away from the destiny God had purposed for me. The man I kept thinking I had a chance with almost destroyed my life. I mean really destroyed my life. He was counterfeit. Ever met one of those? I had heard about counterfeits but it took me a very long time to finally see that he was one. It seemed that every time I felt joy in my life, this man robbed me of it. I knew that God did not intend for me, His daughter, to live in such misery. I knew that this was not abundant living. I allowed and asked this guy to come back into my life many times. I guess you could say I really wanted him to be my husband. Every time I decided to get him out of my life it would be temporary. In doing so, I was really separating myself from what God had in store for me. Remember what I taught you in the beginning, that the enemy reminds us of the good things. He fails to remind us of how we were hurt, or how we cried. We start to believe in him, when whom we need to believe in is God who says, "I took that man out of your life for a reason. He's no good for you. He wasn't good for you then, and he's not good for you now." Praise God for that revelation. One day it hit me, after many years, and finally, I never went back or let him back into my life again.

It was when I finally accepted my singleness, that the Lord opened my eyes. I learned how I needed to live my life as a single woman. I learned to be "Single and Satisfied!" As soon as I became happy with where I was, I saw things that were very sad and broke my heart. I saw women rushing into marriage for all the wrong reasons. I promised myself that I would never compare myself to them and began to speak the following words to myself: "So what, women have husbands that can do many things, I am single but I have God and he can do all things." Another thing I saw was that many women put their lives on hold while they waited for their knight in shining armor to ride into their lives. These women feel that their present could not be permanent, let alone a long time. Without knowing for sure they live life like it is a temporary condition. They wait on a husband to be able to do so many things that they could do themselves. They rent instead of buy, they do not make their house a home, they never cook, and instead they eat out all the time. These women do not save, or take vacations. They do not learn how to manage a household. Why? Because they think they will soon have a husband to do it for them.

I was single for many years and realized that I could be single for a long time to come so I started to do all these things by myself. I ask you, "Are you one of these women?" Have you put your life on hold until you can find someone to hold? Think about it. Just the thought of it is very sobering, but it does happen. Don't let it happen to you. To live your life as though the state you are in is temporary is not a very rewarding way to live. For many years I had put my life on hold, I did set realistic time goals, but nevertheless, I had put my life on hold. I bought my first house when I was 29 years old, I was one year into that relationship which broke my heart, this was before God had entered in to my life, and in my home, and I lived in sin. I figured that "my house" was "my house" a starter home I purchased myself. I thought that at the end of five years we would be married and have enough money saved up to buy a house together, a house that was bigger, nicer and "ours." Well after five years the man in my life had enough money and surprised me by buying himself a house in another city. He didn't even think about helping me buy "our" house. It's so funny; I helped him select everything for his house, the colors, the tile, and the carpet. It was all for him and the woman he would end up sharing it with, whom by the way did not turned out to be me. Right away I decided that I would no longer wait, that I would get that nicer, bigger home I wanted all by myself. Never mind if I didn't have anyone to get it with. I would buy it myself and I did just that. Let me tell you it was such a rewarding feeling. I knew that someday I still wanted to get that house "together" with my husband. I wanted to share the excitement of picking out tile, paint, carpet and furniture with him. I wanted a husband to share my home with, but I couldn't just sit around and wait for him to come for that to happen. You know God made a promise to us. He promised that he came so that we could have life and have it more abundantly. He didn't promise that he came to give us life more abundantly when we were married. He just promised to give us life more abundantly. I don't know about you, but to me that means I can have life abundantly while I am single.

The thief comes only to steal, and kill and destroy. I came that they may have life and have it abundantly.
John 10:10

It is an awesome feeling to be single and trust entirely in the Lord. The feeling compares to no other. I am talking about the feeling of peace that passes all understanding. When you know that you know that He will not let you down, or disappoint you, he will never leave your or forsake you, or break his promises to you. God will forgive you, He will comfort you, and he will protect you. God will care for you, he will provide for you, he will guide you, he will help you in all ways and he will always love you. Now girlfriend think about it, isn't that what you want from a man? I tell you if you don't have God in your life, the perfect husband, the one that will never, ever let you down; who's already shown you amazing love and grace, how could you trust in another man that is not perfect and sure to let you down?

I must admit that my changing and enjoying life was not entirely up to me. I had some help. I have always been a reader and started reading about being single before I even started writing. There were four books I would like to acknowledge for being life-changing during this time

in my life and once God put the desire in my heart....
motivated me to write my own book once God had put
the desire in my heart. These books were "*A Lady, Her
Lover, Her Lord*" by T.D. Jakes, "*Lady in Waiting*" by Debbie
Jones & Jackie Kendall, also "*Get a Love Life*", "*How to Have
a Love Affair With God*", and "*What to do Until Love Finds
You*", all by Michelle McKinney Hammond. All these books
ministered to me and made me praise God for giving me
the time to be single.

No Limits Here

Have you not learned yet that when you resist to
submitting to God and make him your Lord, what you are
really doing, is seeking to have life your way? By having
life your way you are setting restrictions for yourself
and limiting what God can and wants to do for you.
Girlfriend, don't you know our God is a God who has no
limits? Why in heaven would you want to limit what He
can do for you? If He has you in a position right now of
singleness, trust that he is preparing you. "Preparing me
for what?" you might ask. What can I say, the possibilities
are unlimited. Why would you want to settle for anything
less? So many times "the world" believes the idea that one
can be content with things that are outside the body. They
think that if they had just one more thing, they would be
happy. This is so far from the truth. The truth of the matter
is that God's idea of contentment begins and ends within,
not with anything on the outside, success, a job, a house,
a car, money, or a husband. We will get more into this in
a later chapter. For now, know that nothing, absolutely
nothing outside of GOD can make you feel content. If you
were thinking there was someone or something, let it go
now. There is no one or no thing that can make you feel
content. In fact, all it will do is limit you. On the contrary,

if you are content with God, if you allow him to complete you, there is no limit.

Imagine what God could do for a couple, for a marriage, if they were both complete in Him before they got together. With no limits set, the possibilities are endless. Think of a man and a woman, both of them thinking they just need one or two more things to make them happy. That's a max of four things as a couple. You decide which one is better? Now think if neither had a limit and the possibilities were limitless, how much could you have as a couple? Get the point?

> *Ask and it will be given to you, search and you Will find, knock and the door shall be open, for Everyone who asks receives, and everyone who Searches finds and for everyone who knocks the Door will be opened.*
> *Matthew 7:7-8*

Alone but not Lonely

Now maybe you are tired of being single because you are tired of being alone. Let me be real here, there are worst things than being alone, or have you never found yourself with someone yet felt like you were alone? Honey, talk about a feeling that can be devastating, I have felt it. I have had a man in my life, in my home, lying in bed right next to me and still felt the loneliness that has made me cry myself to sleep. It wasn't until I turned to God and accepted Him, not only as my Savior but also as my Lord that I understood I could be alone and still not be lonely. What a wonderful feeling; to know that the love of your life is always there in spirit. Forget about the flesh, having someone in person does not mean that you won't feel alone. I assure you my friend, if your life is not made strong by your relationship with your Lord, or if you do not have your life centered on him, you will enter into relationship after relationship for the wrong reason. Each time attempting to fulfill, a void no earthly man can fill. Each time hurting more than the time before.

I cannot say enough about how good it is for a woman to spend time alone. It is during this time alone that she can search her soul and accept herself. Build a strong relationship with herself, and learn to love herself. It is after all this that she will have become a gift for her husband. So girl, enjoy your single season. Do not get out of the order of God. If you do, you will be in trouble. Your time as a single woman is a very important and unique opportunity in your life. You must use it wisely. Be careful of what you do with it, for the seeds you sow will be the seeds you reap in your married life. Use this time to further your walk with God. During this time talk to Him, listen to Him, worship Him, and allow Him to heal you. As a single woman you need to understand the benefits of your calling during this season. This is your season, water you garden and nourish it while you prepare yourself for a great harvest. As you grow closer to the Lord, you will lose focus on having a mate, because you will feel His presence in your life. With him, you will no longer feel alone. This will give you the opportunity to, carefully and patiently, really check out the men that come into your life, to see if they are what you really want. Know that not until you have delighted yourself in The Lord and he has seen your faithfulness will he give you the desires of your heart.

Delight yourself in the Lord and He shall give you the desires of your heart.
Psalm 37:4

Let's Talk Real Intimacy

I have already stated how I have become a woman who is successfully single and enjoying the love affair I have with my Lord. Oh, how sweet it is! Experiencing intimacy with him is greater than anything I have experienced with any man on earth. Of course, I am talking about real intimacy. What is real intimacy? Think about it, the Lord will never be so tired that he won't stay up and chat with you when you can't seem to be able to get to sleep. He will sit at the edge of your tub while you are taking a bath and he will listen to you pour your heart out to Him. Now, isn't that real intimacy? Isn't that what you are looking for in a real man? Stop looking girl, you already have it. Believe me when I tell you that once you have experienced intimacy that way, your whole perspective on life and the season you are in will change. You will begin to appreciate the time you have, those moments become special; you will enjoy being yourself and by yourself. When you are happy and content single, you will be able to relax because you won't be in such a hurry to give up that time you have with your Lord in order to spend time with a man. Once you enter a love affair with God, and make him your Lord, you will become choosy about the men you spend time with. After all, when you spend time with a man you are making an investment. No one ever makes an investment without expecting anything in return, or do they? I tell you intimacy with God will prompt you to guard your heart more carefully and to not just give it away. It will make you acquire patience and to quietly accept God's timing.

My advice to you is to use your single time to settle any issues that bring stress to your life. Use it to clean out and empty the closets of memories that are in your mind. Believe me if you don't, you will not be happy when you are married. Issues settled and closets emptied while you are still single will limit unnecessary baggage that so many unhealed women bring into relationships. Ultimately it ends up destroying their marriages. Believe me when I tell you that waiting is meant to prevent you from hurting or from hurting others. It is not meant for you to hurt. So many people marry while they are still hurting hoping the person they marry will heal them. That just doesn't happen. Has it not entered your mind that if you can't fix yourself, no one else will either? It needs to! What happens when women get married expecting to be healed is they end up still hurting, and hurting the men they marry. Hurting people are bound to hurt people or allow others to hurt them. Haven't you ever heard that? Hurt will happen if you get ahead of God and do not wait, do not let that happen.

Be a Grand Gift

When you have worked hard to be a "good woman", a "Ms. Proverbs 31" woman nothing less than a "good man" will suffice for you. A "so-so" man just won't do. If you have not heard about Ms. Proverbs 31, that's okay, I'll be introducing her to you in the next chapter. Back to the man, make sure that you are in a position where you will be able to distinguish between the two (the good man and the "so-so" man.) It's very important that you learn this, for the enemy will send counterfeits your way and try to deceive you. He's very good and if you are not careful you will be fooled. Pray to God that He will lead you to the man He has for you and that He will not let you allow the enemy to put a counterfeit in your way. Ask God to reveal Himself to you and speak to your heart. For there will be many times when your eyes can't see and your ears can't listen, but your heart can feel.

Do not spend time preparing yourself to be a grand gift just so that you give it away and accept any old gift in return. I am talking "king" material here. After all, you are a princess, when you get married you should become a queen so nothing less than a King will do. Girlfriend, you have to ensure that the man you are getting is also a grand gift. Even though many of us would not admit it, let's be real, when you exchange gifts, you expect one back that's at minimum the same value as the one you have given, right? Then why would you accept less in return for the greatest gift you will ever give, yourself?

The Lord's greatest delight is for you to allow Him to make sweet love to you. He wants for you to feel His loving arms wrapped around you. He wants you to feel His strength and His peace. He wants to hear you proclaim, "Lord, I am yours, I surrender to you. Do with me what you want." Once you have surrendered you life to Him, you will begin to see things happen the way you want them to.

You're Very Own Husband

But because of cases of sexual immorality, each man should have His own wife and each woman should have her own husband
1 Corinthians 7:2

Okay ladies; remember in the beginning of this chapter, I mentioned how every woman should have her own husband. Let me tell you what I really meant by that, what I mean is that a woman should not have another's woman husband—but her own. I am specific about the word "own" because many women, especially single women have husbands but not their own. I am reminded of a story I read a while back. In the story, a very independent, career-minded woman who did not want to be married met a married man. She began an affair with this man. After many years she found herself in love and with her biological clock ticking and she wanted him to be her husband. The man "loved" his wife and would not leave her. The "woman" decided she wanted to have a baby and allowed herself to become pregnant. Much to her surprise the man still wouldn't leave his wife. In conversation with her best friend she cried out and said, "All I wanted was a husband." Her friend responds to this by saying, "Well you wanted a husband, you got a husband. You never said he had to be your own husband." Good huh?

It saddens me to have to get into this subject, but I'm just being real. You have probably seen adultery take place in the church. If you haven't seen it, I hate to break it to you, but you must beware of the fact that just because you don't see it or don't want to admit it, it does not mean it is not there. Let me tell you something just because a woman is in the church does not mean she's not a loose woman. Women, especially single women know a good thing when they see it. Believe me they are zooming in on good men, many times with the goal to make them theirs. They watch for those husbands who seem to be neglected and not given the attention they need. Sometimes wives are so into the church and ministry that they put their husbands on the back burner. These poor wives never realize their husbands need them, and all along someone is there ready to make him feel the way she used to make him feel. This woman can be married, unhappily married of course, but most of the time she's single. As you live your life single do not allow yourself to be so vulnerable that one day you find yourself suddenly committing adultery. Follow some advice on how to avoid this. First, do not become friends with a married man if you cannot be friends with his wife. Second, do not let a married man talk to you negatively about his wife or about how unhappy his marriage is. Third, for sure, never have intimate conversation with a married man,

Committing adultery is a big no-no. If you have already been an adulterer, remember your sins are washed away. You might think you have never committed sin, so you think! If you have committed adultery you my dear have committed a grave sin. Very shamefully, I admit that a long time ago before the Lord came into my life and I got planted in a church, when I was out there, I messed with a couple married men. It was never my intent to be with a married man, I didn't know the things I know now, I was very vulnerable and things just happened. Once I had been with a married man, it was never my intent to make them "mine". There was one I wanted to be mine. One who didn't even tell me he was married until I had fallen in love and given myself to him. Luckily, a wife never found out I was talking to her husband, nonetheless I coveted other women's husband and I knew.

If you are committing this grave sin, stop right now! Repent and allow God to forgive you. Start doing the following. First don't just pray for a husband, pray for your own husband. Second, while you are single, focus on your Lord and give him all the attention he deserves. When you get married you could give your husband the attention he deserves. Won't have to worry about another woman lurking around, ready to give him what only you should give.

Finally, a Love Story

Only when you have become what God wants you to become will YOU have what he wants you to have, not before then. "What am I saying here?" It's simple. Use this time to become that woman God wants you to become. Then and only then, will he choose to provide you with a husband. A husband that will be better than anyone you would have chosen on your own. As a matter of fact, better than anyone you would have imagined. Don't push, manipulate or force things to happen before their time, you've been alone this long, why rush now? Enjoy your season until God chooses for it to be over. While in your season, do not attempt to write your own love story. Let God write it for you. I promise you it will be better than anything you can do yourself. Parents always want what is best for their children. What makes you think God wants different for His children? When God wants you married, He will carefully and strategically maneuver people, circumstances, places and events in your life that will make that "divine encounter" possible. You have nothing to be afraid of because, it will happen. There is nothing you have to do except become what he wants you to become. Surrender to His will; learn to be patient and whallah….let things happen. At the appointed time, God will bring to you that one good and perfect man, He's been saving for you. The one that will truly make you happy and end your single season. I don't know about you but just knowing that is definitely worth the wait and encourages to live "Single, Successful and Satisfied!"

Do not stir up or awaken love until it is ready.
Song of Songs 2:7

Final Word

Having been a single woman most of my life and not knowing that I could be happy where I was, my heart really goes out to single women who seem to walk in denial of where they are in their lives. My heart especially goes out to the type of single women I have witnessed first hand, who live their lives on hold while they wait until their husbands arrive. These women sadden me because they allow life to slip by them. Never having experienced the incredible opportunity, the gift they have been given of being a single woman. It has given me great pleasure to write this chapter. To share with women about filling the void that is in their heart and about how they could be alone and not lonely, how being alone can be so much better than being with someone and feeling lonely. It has been a pleasure to write about being able to live life joyfully and fulfilled while being single. My desire is that you have come to realize that time is too precious to be wasted. In Jesus' name I pray that I have touched women and simply my testifying on how my life has changed and how I enjoy being a single woman I have turned around lives. I hope you have enjoyed the ride we have taken in this chapter, as I shared my own personal life, my works, my counsel and the realization I finally came to. I hope you have learned from my host of secrets, thoughts and revelations. To love the here and now and to know that there is a reason for the season, and not rush into things. Take care of your father's business, prepare yourself to be married, be anxious for nothing and instead be patient. Most importantly to live your life "Single and Satisfied"

Prayer

Heavenly Father, thank you for this season you have ordained in my life and the precious gift of time you have entrusted in me Lord. Let me never take this blessing for granted; instead help me to use this time wisely and to maximize every moment. I ask you to help me to be faithful to you during this time and accept willingly the work you want to do in my life. Help me to work for your glory and purpose and make me the woman you meant for me to be. I thank you Lord for showing me how full and complete life as a single woman can be and for allowing me to be alone, but not feel lonely. Father God, I ask that you continue to prepare me to be a blessing in every area to the man you have destined for me. I ask you to help me not to judge by physical appearance and material wealth, but by what is really important, the heart and a passion that burns for you. I ask you to give me the gift of discernment to recognize the hidden motives of men that the enemy brings into my life so that I am never deceived by what is not of you. Lord, guard my thoughts, make them pure, and keep my heart safe in the palm of your hand. Help me Lord to rest in your love and wait peacefully until you bring into my life your best for me, the one that will manifest your love for me in Jesus' Name. Amen

Secrets of Success

Success is only success because it has been achieved through struggle.

Those who are attentive to a matter will prosper (Proverbs 16:20)

Not everyone can handle success that is why not everyone has it.

Successful people are passionate people who love what they do.

Having passion but no goal to focus it on will not make you successful.

You must be willing to pay the price it will cost you to attain success.

Success requires pursuit that is persistent.

The appetite of workers works for them; their hunger urges them on. (Proverbs 16:26)

If success was easy to achieve everyone would be successful.

Successful people possess intense desire.

Desire and determination is what drives people to be successful.

To have success and no one to share it with is a lonely thing.

Success is bound to bring about stress.

To be successful you must never quit.

You have only yourself to blame if you lack success.

It is not realistic to think success will come without adversity.

Successful people do not allow obstacles to become excuses for them to quit.

You could have riches, power, and fame and still not have success.

What constitutes success? She has achieved success who has lived well; laughed often, and loved much; who has gained the respect of intelligent people and the love of little children; who has filled and niche and accomplished her task; who has left the world better than she found it; who has always looked for the best in others and given the best she had.
- Bessie Anderson Stanley

6
An Irresistible Woman

*R*ejoice and give thanks and praise to God for making you a woman, for it is a blessing and such a wonderful thing. In case you didn't know, in God's masterpiece of creation, you are a very important, integral part. For that reason, he has fashioned you very delicately, fearfully, wonderfully and purposefully. That you are a woman is a magnificent gift. Don't get me wrong, a man is a wonderful thing, a magnificent gift, but a woman…. there's a certain something about her. She is so many things. She's a work of art, a creature of rare beauty, a priceless jewel. As a woman, you must know what you are worth beyond a shadow of a doubt. You are precious, unique, exquisite, a treasured possession, a prized wonder, a fine piece. In the eyes of your father, the King you are a beloved and righteous princess. Never underestimate how valuable the man God has for you and will find you to be, your price will be far above rubies. He will appreciate you and the way you have prepared yourself for him. When the right man comes along, he will know he has found a rare and special thing. That man will appreciate, cherish, and honor you. He will so badly want to make you his wife, that just like Esther you will become his queen, and he will see you as "an irresistible woman."

Miss Proverbs 31

As a woman your goal should be to become a Miss Proverbs 31 woman. To be this kind of woman, you must be many, many things. Not only that, but most amazingly, you must be all these things at the same time. We'll get more into that in a bit, but for now, think of the Proverbs 31 Woman. Talk about having it going on, wow, this woman was all that and a bag of chips. She was an organizer, a homemaker, a hard worker, and a provider. She had dignity, wisdom, and grace. She was virtuous, which by the way means excellent. She was noble, courageous, gentle, strong, supportive, inspiring, nurturing, and she had a trait that brought her praise, she feared the Lord. The list goes on and on.

> *Charm is deceitful, and beauty is vain, but a woman who fears the Lord is to be praised.*
> *Proverbs 31:30*

This woman was an absolute 10. There was something very special about her, she was second to none. Now girlfriend, isn't that what you want to be? Believe me, if a man finds all that in a woman, he will feel captivated and left mesmerized. I don't know about you, but I sure want to be that. I love the Proverbs 31 woman, for she undoubtedly had her act together. All that she was, made her an absolutely amazing, admirable, charming, elegant, fabulous, incredible and lovely woman. My advice to you is to get to know this woman. Let her be your mentor, allow her to challenge you. For you girlfriend are no less amazing that she was, therefore if you wanted to put your all into it, you my dear could very easily become her.

I am definitely a testimony to women all over. No matter what you have done, no matter where you have been, you can be a woman of excellence. To be a woman of excellence doesn't mean you had to grow up in a condominium, have had a silver spoon in your mouth, or be a university graduate. Oh no! Take it from me. A girl who grew up in the projects in the ghetto, a child on welfare and food stamps. I used to stand in cheese lines and had to go into the military because I wasn't smart enough or rich enough to get an education. For a long time, I lived my life out there, wild. One day I met the Lord, I submitted myself to him, realized my purpose, and became a woman of excellence. I promise you, you too have it in you. Remember you are fearfully and wonderfully made. You have what you need inside of you, so let the woman of excellence that's in you take charge, and become a Miss Proverbs 31.

The Real Sense of Beauty

Okay let's talk about something we are all interested in—beauty. As women, we are fascinated by beauty. You know what I mean. As women, we spend money on makeup, clothing, fashion accessories and jewelry. We spend money getting our hair styled, our eyebrows waxed and arched, our nails done, our skin tanned, our muscles toned. Some of you who have had the money, I'm sure have even spent money on getting something nipped or getting your tummy tucked. Maybe, you've thought about injecting collagen in your lips, getting your nose done, or maybe even getting a boob job. I was not being happy with myself; I wanted my nose done and my lips done. If it wasn't because I couldn't stand pain, I would have. Believe it or not I also wanted to gain some weight. I mean I have always been so petite, that when my daughters were 13 & 16, taller and bigger than me, no one could believe I was their mother. I guess you can say I wanted to get big so I could look like a woman. Well, finally I came to the realization, that if God had wanted me to have a smaller nose, bigger lips, and a bigger body he would have given them to me. I realize also that God makes no junk; therefore I was altogether lovely and indeed beautiful. The person he had for me would love and appreciate me just the way I was.

While we are on the subject of beauty, let's go more in depth on what is real beauty. Of course I'm talking about inner beauty. I'm talking about the kind of beauty that no matter what you look like will give you no problem attracting a man. I'm talking about the kind of beauty that radiates from a heart that has been washed by God's blood. So what about this beauty thing, let's get into it! Women, cute, pretty, beautiful. I remember my mother teaching me the different levels of beauty when I was younger. She taught me that a girl was one of those things; cute, pretty, beautiful, or as she use to say in Spanish, Linda, bonita, bella. It didn't hit me until much later in life, that a woman is in fact all those things at different stages of her life. In thinking about my own beauty. I would describe it just that way, cute, pretty, and beautiful. I was cute as a baby, then I went through the stage when I wasn't any of that, not even cute, as a matter of fact, I thought I was ug----ly. I tell you my beauty did not start until very late in life. I wasn't pretty growing up in the least. As a young girl my parents never told me I was beautiful, so I never saw myself the way God saw me--beautiful. I would say I was more like an "ugly duckling,"

I was skinny and as flat as an ironing board. I was very plain, had bad hair and needed braces. In my late teens I was still not what I would call pretty but I gained some weight, had a back if you know what I mean. Also I wore lots of makeup. Now let's be real, how many of us thank God for makeup?

It wasn't till my late 20s that I finally saw myself as "pretty". By this time I had braces and started taking care of my hair. I began working out and weightlifting so I had developed a very nice, firm, guitar-shaped body as my ex-boyfriend used to call it. In my early 30s, I considered myself to be pretty. My "boyfriend" would tell me over and over that I was beautiful, of course what else would he say? Even after hearing it, I really did not see myself that way; although I believed that I was—to him.

It wasn't until I was 35 years old and my "boyfriend" had left me that I saw myself as beautiful. I attribute my beauty to the Lord being in my life. It was He, His grace, peace, and mercy that totally transformed me. I had become beautiful because my beauty was inside. The face, makeup, hair and the body were all just extras that made me even more beautiful. The glow I had seen on women faces when I looked at them before, I could now see on my face when I looked in the mirror. Everyone would tell me I was beautiful, guys and girls. Wow, that is such a great feeling to introduce yourself to a woman and she tells you how beautiful you are. To be sitting alone at a restaurant and out of no where a woman approaches you and tells you "excuse me; I just wanted to tell you, I think you are beautiful." For your friends to see you and greet you with "hey beautiful." I tell you it's a great feeling to be called beautiful because of what you project from the inside. Now that my dear is the real sense of beauty.

> *Let your adornment be the inner self with the lasting beauty of a gentle and quiet spirit, which is very precious in God's sight.*
>
> *1 Peter 3:4*

Beautiful Within

I love that old classic song that went something like this*: You are so beautiful to me can't you see? You're everything I hoped for, you're everything I need. You are so beautiful to me.* I love it because to me it portrays beauty within.

It's very important to know that it is not enough for you to just look beautiful, you must be beautiful within. For what you do, say and think will greatly impact and have more of a lasting impression, than what you look like. I don't care how beautiful you are on the outside; if you don't have it in the inside you just don't have it. Don't you know God put more of what a man wants inside of you than what is on the outside of you? Make sure that the inside looks just as good as the outside. I've got news for you. You might be able to use what you have on the outside to attract him. Yeah every man wants a pretty woman, but that just allows you in. Girlfriend, believe me, if you don't have it on the inside, trust me you will not be allowed to stay. A man will fall in love with you not because of the way you look, but because of the way you make him feel. Don't get me wrong you got to look good, but you don't have to be beautiful according to the world's take on beauty. In God's eyes you are beautiful. The right man that is, the man God has for you will be a manifestation of Him therefore; to him you will be beautiful as well. Ask your male friends, what they consider to be beautiful. Listen to their response, I bet they mention beauty within. I have asked my male friends and created my own little survey. It never fails. Yea, a man loves to have a trophy he can parade with, but when it comes down to the nitty-gritty, he will fall in love with you because of the beauty you have within and because of the way he feels when he is with you. I tell you girlfriend, if you don't have it in the inside of you, how do you think you are going to give it to him? You need to realize and hold on to the fact that for a man, what's inside of you is even more important than what is on the outside of you, I am of course talking about a real man. A man of GOD who knows about substance. A man who wants to see a wife he could spend his life with, not a pretty young thing he could have a fling with. Now that doesn't go for the men of the world. A man in the world will always be more interested in the things of the world. So physical beauty is definitely more of a hit with them. Of course you do not want a man who's in the world do you?

Just because you are beautiful on the outside today, does not mean you will be beautiful on the outside tomorrow. Over time much of the outside will change, that's right, I hate to break it to you. Things will change and you will not always look as good as you do. As you get older, your hair will turn gray, circles will appear under your eyes, the wrinkles will come, and your tight belly won't be as tight, your perky boobs will begin to sag, but what's inside of you, in your heart and in your soul, will remain the same forever.

When I say beautiful I am really saying beautiful on three levels at the same time, your soul, mind and physical body. That means what you feel, what you think and how you look. All three at work are incredibly enticing. One out of whack and you can totally turn a man off. Think about it, or what have you never met a man who was tall, dark & handsome. He seems to have it going on, that is until he opens his mouth. What came out of his mouth, it wasn't very pretty. I know I have. Do you think that women can't be like that and make that same kind of impression on a man? Of course we can, I have met beautiful women who when they open their mouth turn ugly. What, do you not think that the same exact thing can happen to men? It does. I have heard them say just that "she was beautiful, until she opened her mouth." This leads me to another very important point, your tongue. I mean your words, the way you talk. Girl you need to talk right. Be positive, no cursing, and no negative talk. Nothing turns off a man more than that, we'll get more into this in the next chapter.

> *Hear, for I will speak noble things, and from my lips will come what is right; for my mouth will utter truth; wickedness is an abomination to my lips . All the words of my mouth are righteous; there is nothing twisted or crooked in them.*
> *Proverbs 8:6-8*

Okay now that we've addressed that, let's talk about how a woman should look. A woman definitely needs to pay attention to her physical body, and her sense of style (how she dresses, accessorizes, how she carries herself, how she walks, how she talks, how she stands, how she sits). Remember that men are visual and are stimulated by what they see. No matter how spiritual he is and how much he says he doesn't care about looks, let me tell you something, he's lying. Don't let him fool you, he's a man. If there's one thing we know about men it's that they are visual beings. Being visual means he will be attracted and stimulated by what he sees on the outside, therefore it's not enough that you are spiritual and got it going on in the inside. You must also have it going on, in the outside to get his attention.

So maybe you don't think you are beautiful, who told you that? Whoever it was, they lied. I am here to tell you that God sees you as beautiful and if he sees it that settles it, so get with it. Know that no matter how you look on the outside, even if you don't think you are beautiful, you can be beautiful because of how you look in the inside. I think I have made myself clear as far as the "outside" look. You need to look good. I am not saying you have to look like Ms. Universe, oh no not at all. I am just saying to look good, you can do that no matter how you think you look. Get your hair done, dress up, and please wear some makeup. Go and get a makeover you can usually get it done complimentary at any department store. Whatever you do make sure that the colors look good on you. I remember when I was younger I put purple and pink eye shadow on my eyes and purple on my lips. Wow what a sight. As I got older I wore more neutral, softer colors, what a difference it made in the way I looked.

Okay, another important point is intellect and being well-cultured. "What does she mean by that?" You are probably asking huh? Here it goes. You need to have some smarts, even if you haven't been to college. Girl have some common sense and read some books.

Keep up with the news, watch sports, learn countries and culture, familiarize yourself with politics, music, art, and movies. You should be able to talk about everything. Know a little bit about everything. As a woman you have to be able to carry a conversation, and one day you'll be able to intellectually stimulate your man. Alright, I have shared a lot here, and I now want to get something straight. I am by no means underestimating spirituality, I am just trying to make a point that beauty combined with intelligence and spirituality equals desirability. I am talking about the type of desirability that makes a woman irresistible. I tell you that's what you want to be for the man God has chosen for you. You want to be irresistible. So how else do you become irresistible? Let me break it down for you my dear, being irresistible is really all about how you present yourself.

Learn to present yourself in such a way that when you walk into a room people will look at you and ask amongst themselves "Who is she?" "I want what she's got!" Let this be done not because of your beautiful face, or your perfectly shaped body, because of the stunning dress you are wearing. Let them ask it simply because of how you present yourself. Because of the confidence in which you carry yourself with, how you speak and the character you display. I tell you nothing could be more attractive and attention grabbing and make you feel better than to be beautiful from the inside out.

A Woman of Balance

Having a relationship with her Lord and Savior and finding contentment in being a single woman, is difficult. Yet the most important task a single woman must achieve in her life in preparation for what God has in store for her future is to find balance. There is no question, as a Christian woman you must always be in the pursuit of balance, for without it even if you have God you will still feel like you are incomplete. Only when you have achieved balance will you feel totally complete.

Now balance is difficult to achieve, yes it is, it can even be challenging, but it can be achieved. Think about this thought, I once heard my pastor say "if the devil can't make you bad, he'll make you busy." I remember raising my hand up and proclaiming "YES." You know what I am talking about, huh? Well with God in your life, the pursuit of balance can be accomplished. To achieve balance in your life you must be creative and make time to replenish yourself. Read a book, get a massage, go for a walk or get away to a spa or the mountains. Do whatever you have to do to replenish yourself. If you don't, for sure someone is bound to drain you dry or you will cause yourself to burnout.

The difficult aspect of balance for a woman is not being successful in all her roles. Most importantly, as a woman you must be recognized as who you are and not just the roles you play. Just as God so many times is known for the gifts he gives and not as giver, you can be known for what you do and not who you are.

Like the woman in Proverbs 31, a woman can have and do it all. That's right, the purposed-driven life. The perfect husband, family, the gorgeous house, the dependable, friends, the "dream" job, serventhood, financial security, hopes and dreams. I think I covered it all, didn't I? Anyway she can, but she cannot first without God, or second, without balance.

Think about the roles you play. Now picture this scenario of a multi-role woman. She is a business woman and provider who gets up at the crack of dawn to fix herself up and head out to corporate America where she might run a company, manage people, conducts board meetings, present proposals and then close deals. She then turns into a housewife and mother who comes home to be a cook and prepare a meal for the family. She is a mother who must bathe her children and then put them to sleep. Then she is a housewife who must clean the kitchen and wash the dishes after dinner. She is then a woman who sinks into a bubble bath, listens to soft music while she relaxes, then becomes a lover who jumps into bed to make love to her husband, who's been relaxing for hours. Can anybody identify with this woman? Of course you can!

A good start to becoming balanced is possessing the ability to just say no. I don't know why, maybe because of our nurturing nature, but we women have a challenge with saying no. We just want to be able to do it all. Girlfriend, let me tell you something, sometimes you just need to be able to raise your hand up and say no. Do not get upset with anyone but yourself, when you think you are doing too much. It is completely up to you to let people know you need a break. If you don't tell them they won't know so you can't blame them. I tell you, you can't do it all, there is just no possible way, it can't happen. Being a mother of teenagers I can attest to this. There was a point in my life when every single night there was something going on. I remember driving an hour home from work to pick up one of my girls to go right back the way I just came from. I would take her to Praise & Worship Team practice, the next night it was my other daughter who had Track or Basketball practice. When there wasn't practice there would be a meet, a game, finals, a tournament or something. Then on top of all that, there was church, leadership meetings, bible study, home group, teaching, fundraisers, my quiet time, "movie or game night" at the house with my girls or night out with the "girls." I tell you I had God in my life, he was the center of it, but with everything else, my life was a complete disarray and sometimes I just couldn't even feel him around. Get this, in the midst of all this; I wanted my husband to find me. It was so funny, I would be rushing to get the girls somewhere, stressing out, and I would yell right there in the car in front of them, "No wonder God hasn't sent me my husband, he knows I wouldn't have any time for him." I don't know about you, but when my husband comes, I want to be ready for him. I don't want to be doing all kinds of stuff; I want a relationship that is rich, not monotonous. I want to be able to spend time with him, walking with God and with him. I want to communicate with him, love him, and not rush in and out of the house throwing kisses, or as my pastor did, once while he was rushing, he told his wife, "consider yourself kissed." Oh no!!!! I want to be balanced in all I do, stop doing what I cannot do and prepare a safe haven that is free of clutter, stress and everything else that comes with doing too much. I want to be balanced. I know it's hard but it can be done.

A Woman Well-Kept

Remember God has fashioned you delicately, fearfully, wonderfully and purposefully.

I praise you for I am fearfully and wonderfully made.
Wonderful are your works that I know very well.
Psalm 139:14

Girlfriend it is very important that you take care of yourself and look and act like a woman who is well-kept. If you do, once the man that God has for you finds you, he will recognize you as the part that's missing from him. You my dear will be that missing rib. You will be the woman he's been waiting for. I say waiting because this man honey, he has not been looking, he has been waiting and will know you are the one as soon as you arrive. This leads me to another point, be careful when a man tells you he's been looking for you. If a man has been looking, there's no telling how many women there have been.

As a woman that is well-kept, you have it going on not only when it comes to knowing some stuff but taking care of stuff as well. That's okay if you don't have intellect, but at least have some smarts. Believe me a guy does not want a girl who knows nothing. Girl, you have to be interesting, you have to know a little bit about everything, know what's going on in the world, know politics, culture, music, movies, sports, and be able to carry a conversation on anything that comes up. So pleassssee, get an education and by that I don't necessarily mean you have to go to college to do it. You don't need to spend a lot of money. With the world of Internet today it is easy to get some knowledge. You can also go to the library, bookstore, watch the news in the privacy of your own home, or whatever, just get some knowledge about stuff. I tell you what a man wants to find a woman who has some smarts, but he also wants to find a woman who takes care of things. This man will have no problem trusting you if you do.

A woman who is well-kept takes care of her home, including the yard. Even if you are like me and have to pay someone to do it. Also, the kitchen, that's right the kitchen. That means you need to know how to cook. If you don't know how, I suggest you buy yourself a cookbook and don't just put it up on some shelf, use it. Also, as a woman who is well-kept not only do you take care of your home, but you take care of yourself. I mean your clothes, finances, car maintenance, personal records, medical and dental needs. Girlfriend, you do not want for your man to find you when your stuff's a mess. You do not want for him to come into your life and have to take care of a whole bunch of things. Have your stuff together before he finds you. It will make the time while you wait go by faster.

It's sad to see how many women want to be taken care of, and for some man to come into their lives and do everything for them. Let me tell you something. You need to take care of yourself and your own matters and be prepared to be a helper to your mate when he comes. Girl you don't want a man who takes care of you, I mean you do want a man who takes care of you but one who does because he wants to, not because he needs to. You know what I mean? The type of man who wants a woman who needs him to take care of her has issues. A true man, one who walks with the Lord, takes care of business is self-confident and is drawn to a woman just like him. Of course, I know this because I have known the man who wants to be needed by a woman. He is attracted to a weak woman, the one that can not do things for herself. That's the kind of man I was with. The type of man that I having my stuff together made him feel threatened. This man, even when he assumes all responsibilities will not make you happy. You see he won't be happy for long. He doesn't feel needed; therefore, he will never be happy himself. Believe me, the right man when he meets a woman who is well-kept will see how she can challenge him, enhance him, and make him a better person. She will be irresistible to him.

Freedom through Submission

Freedom through submission! Now that sounds kind of ironic, maybe even unbelievable, but it's true, believe it, there is great freedom through submission. Many are the women who are offended, even insulted by this word. These women are too independent and too strong to submit. They would rather bear all responsibility that comes with life on their own, when in actuality; submission was designed to set them free from the burden of so much responsibility. Understand that to submit by no means, suggest that you are less of a woman. In God's order submission is essential.

Practice submitting by surrendering to God and His will every day. Think about it, God submits to us every day, or does he force us to do things His way? Of course not, he gives us the ability to choose. If God who is greater and bigger than us can submit to us, how dare we question the command in the bible that tells us to submit?

Wives be subject to your husbands as you are to the Lord. For the Husband, is the head of the wife just as Christ is the head of the church, the body of which he is the Savior. Just as the church is subject to Christ, so also wives ought to be, in everything to their husbands.
Ephesians 5:22

An independent woman is crafty enough at being submissive without losing herself. This is vital to her well-being, being successful and being a woman of excellence. It is very sad to see the women who lose their womanhood because they can not submit. They assume the role of leadership they were not meant to assume. They become miserable and unhappy trying to be the man they wouldn't let their husband become. Are you one of these women? I know I was for a very long time. Let me give you details on why I was challenged to submit and why I assumed a role that was not for me. My reasons might open your eyes and help you to submit, more importantly to be free.

Wives, in the same way, accept the authority of your husbands, so that even, if some of them do not obey the word, they may be won over without, a word by their wives' conduct.
1 Peter 3:1

There is an order to submission. Man submits to God and then woman submits to man. The willingness to be able to submit of course depends on the trust and respect you have for the person you are submitting to as a leader, and his own submission. I mean to submit to your husband, you must respect the walk he has with God and you must be able to trust his judgment and decision making. So think about it and ask yourself before you get into a relationship too seriously. Can I see this man as the leader of my household? Do I respect this man's walk with God? Do I trust this man with his decision-making? When he becomes my husband will I trust him to do the right thing when it comes to my family? Does this man submit to God? Rest assured if you can't answer these questions affirmatively you will be challenged and see rough bumpy roads ahead. Take it from me; I couldn't answer those questions with a yes. I couldn't see the man in my life submitting to God; therefore I could not see him as a leader. I thought "he can't even make right decisions for his own life and for his kids, how could he for me, for mine." I became the leader, I made decisions, I made plans, I paid the bills, and I took care of everything. Let me tell you it's not a great feeling, it's a burden that can cause you to stress out, not only that, but also lose respect, admiration and trust. Those are things that you need in order to submit and have a successful relationship. I must say this, in the bible, it clearly states that a wife is to submit to her husband, regardless if he is submitting or not.

We women were not designed to operate that way in a relationship. I just couldn't submit to someone who wasn't walking with God, for I knew that he was not capable of making right decisions. For the longest time after our relationship was over, I blamed myself, I thought I was wrong. I really beat myself up, and I would say, "That's what you get for not submitting." In actuality it was him who was not submitting to God, therefore getting us out of order. Of course I was challenged. It was when I became single that I really dedicated myself to learning about submission, and gaining the willingness to be able to do it. I challenged myself to prepare for I did not want this to be a hindrance with my husband in the future. Then to my amazement, it's like God spoke to me and let me know "when I bring you the right man, the one I have destined for you to spend your life with, you will be willing to submit, for this man will be righteous, and have wisdom, he will walk with me, he'll consider your needs before his own needs, he will love you with all that is within him, and he will never leave you astray". Amen!!! Was all I could say?

It is very important to realize that when a woman does not submit to the leadership of her husband, the house will get out of order. The same goes when a man does not assume the leadership role. So go ahead, get things in order submit, and be free

The Garden of Life

Remember the concept I introduced to you in one of the earlier chapters about your life being a private garden, and you its gardener? Well let's return to that. Women you need to think of your life like if it was a garden, and you're its gardener. You must have rich soil for you will cause lives to be rich. In order to do this you must guard your garden with all that is within you. You must be extremely careful with the seeds you plant in it for what you sow or allow others to sow into it, you will reap. There is a rule of seedtime and harvest that absolutely no one can escape.

When it comes to your garden, every circumstance, acquaintance, friendship, affair and love encounter will plant something in it. People will to plant weeds in your life merely with their words so you have to be utmost diligent in regards to your relationships and what you allow others to speak into your life. What is planted will become rooted deep inside the ground and will not easily be uprooted. Be very careful, for whom you speak to will speak to your life. Surround yourself with people who bring life to you, who are positive and encouraging. Refrain from negative people, those who will talk down to you. They will cause danger to your garden and they will plant weeds you will harvest after a time. Most often when the person who planted them is no longer even around to share in your harvest. These weeds will make a mess. Just like a fungus, they will spread throughout your garden and be hard to get rid of.

> *The kingdom of heaven may be compared to someone who sowed good seed in his field; but while everybody was asleep, an enemy came and sowed weeds among the wheat, and then went away. So when the plants came up and bore grain, then the weeds appeared as well.*
>
> *Matthew 13: 24-26*

Think about it, are you not happy with the fruit that you are reaping? Has your heart been dehydrated by hurt? Do you want to grow another kind of fruit? Do you want to irrigate your garden with love? It's simple; change what you are allowing to be sown in your garden. Inventory it and clear any weeds that have been planted by the negative words of others and replace them with the beautiful, uplifting words God has written you in his love letter. Be a good gardener, take care of your garden and watch it blossom.

What a Woman Wants

Once a woman learns who she is and what she is worth, she will know what she wants. What a great thing it is to be a woman who knows her worth in the Lord. She will be mindful of what she deserves, and will demand it and settle for nothing less. This woman will train others how to respect her and how to treat her by the way she respects and treats herself. She will not allow herself to be mistreated or mishandled because she knows she's somebody. This woman will know she's the daughter of a King and must be treated for who she is. Already been there? Where you have been mistreated, and allowed someone to show you no respect? where you let your dignity leave you? That's okay girlfriend, I've been there, done that, and changed it. Since I realized who I was and my worth, there hasn't been anymore of that.

As women we want to be loved, valued, known totally and appreciated for who we are, what we do, not just for what we look like. Don't get me wrong. It's a great feeling and one that gives you a great sense of security to know the man in your life loves the way you look, and has eyes only for you. It's a greater feeling though, when you know that he loves the way you are. Face it, there are a lot of beautiful woman out there, you have to offer him a lot more than looks to keep him.

In the same way, husbands should love their wives as they do their bodies.
He who loves his wife loves himself. For no one ever hates his own body, but he nourishes and tenderly cares for it, just as Christ does for the church.
Ephesians 5:28-29

My dear friend, there are many, many things you need to want in a man and seek in him once you feel God has brought him into your life. Prepare yourself, get a pen and paper because you are about to learn some things and you are going to want to write some of them down. We will cover many things that as a woman you should want your man to have, most important of all you should want a man who not only calls himself a Christian, but who has a heart after God and loves him with passion. Girl, you want a man that is willing to sacrifice and give his life for you. A man who knows what's right and wrong, who you can trust simply because of that. One of my favorite all time songs is a song by Simply Red, called "*If you don't know me by now*", in the song, the guy sings "Now, I know the difference between right and wrong, I ain't going to do anything to break up our happy home." Wow, that's what we want, a guy who knows the difference between right and wrong. Think about it if he loves God he will not want to do him wrong. What does that mean? Simply, it means he'll have your back.

A man who truly has God in him is as close to a perfect man as you will ever meet. This man will have all the good qualities of God in him. He will love, serve, and he will humble himself. He won't lie, he won't cheat and he won't be a sneak. I tell you, I've met all kinds of men out there, now the one that has a heart after God, now that's a king. Honestly there is no more attractive quality than a man whose heart is after God. I don't care how fine the brother is, how much money he has, what he does. When I met this type of guy, everything I thought I wanted, liked and needed went out the window. I'm telling you meeting a man like that changed my life totally. The joy I felt, well I can't really describe it except to say it was joy, pure joy. I tell you a man after God's heart, is what you as a woman wants.

Final Word

I must share with you, that of all my chapters, I really enjoyed writing about being "An Irresistible Woman". In writing about so many things that a woman should be

137

and so many things that she should do, I reacquainted myself with things I already knew, and learned some new things. In reading over this chapter I became excited about the woman I had become. I realized that I was on a journey to becoming a Miss Proverbs 31 Woman. I praised God for all he had done and for giving me the time to work on me. For He has taught me about the real sense of beauty. For giving me beauty within and instilling in me the importance of being balanced and well-kept. I feel refreshed and even challenged to be even more excellent than what God has already made me to be. I sincerely hope that you have learned many things, that these things are not just thing that you read and forget about, but things that you are able to apply to your womanhood. My advice to you now is to strive to be that fearfully, wonderfully made woman God purposed you to be, so that all will look at you and call you "An Irresistible Woman"

Prayer

Heavenly Father, Breathe life into me and make me the virtuous woman you created me to be. I thank you because you made me fearfully and wonderfully. Lord, I release you to make me be a living vessel and walking testimony for you to all that come into my life. Let people look at my life, and know that you are in it, let them say, "I want what she has". Lord, I ask you that you give me inner beauty the kind that is gentle and gracious. Make me a gift to my husband, and enable me to have freedom by having the willingness to submit to him. Father God, I thank you because you know the desires of my heart and will grant them. Lord, I ask that when the time is just right and I have done all that you called me to do, that you will transform me into a good & loyal wife. Let me be willing to honor my husband and address him with respect always, I thank you Lord because the man you have for me, I will trust with his decision making for I will know that he walks with you. Lord, help me with wisdom so that I can make diligent business & career decisions and so that I will always practice balance and seek to refresh myself in your word. Lord, guide me and open up the windows of heaven and pour out blessings in all areas of my life. In Jesus' Name. Amen.

Proverbs 31

A capable wife who can find?
She is far more precious than jewels.
The heart of her husband trusts in her, and he will have no lack of gain.
She does him good and not harm, all the days of her life.
She seeks wool and flax, and works with willing hands.
She is like the ships of the merchant, she brings her food from far away.
She rises while it is still night and provides food for her household and tasks for her servant girls.
She considers a field and buys it; with the fruit of her hands she plants a vineyard.
She girds herself with strength, and makes her arms strong.
She perceives that her merchandise is profitable.
Her lamp does not go out at night.
She puts her hands to the distaff, and her hands hold the spindle.
She opens her hands to the poor, and reaches out her hands to the needy.
She is not afraid of her household when it snows, for all her household are clothed in crimson.
She makes herself coverings; her clothing is fine linen and purple.
Her husband is known in the city gates, taking his seat among the elders of the land.
She makes linen garments and sells them; she supplies the merchant with sashes.
Strength and dignity are her clothing, and she laughs at the time to come.
She opens her mouth with wisdom, and the teaching of kindness is on her tongue.

She looks well to the ways of her household, and does not eat the bread of idleness.

Her children rise up and call her happy; her husband too, and he praises her:

"Many women have done excellently, but you surpass them all."

Charm is deceitful, and beauty is vain, but a woman who fears the Lord is to be praised.

Give her a share in the fruit of her hands, and let her works praise her in the city gates.

Secrets of an Irresistible Woman

1. She is fashioned delicately, fearfully, wonderfully and purposefully.

2. She is a work of art, a creature of rare beauty, a priceless jewel.

3. In the eyes of her father, the King, she is a beloved and righteous Princess.

4. She is a Proverbs 31 Woman.

5. She fears the Lord.

6. Her beauty radiates from the heart.

7. A man will fall in love with her not because of how she looks, but because of how she makes him feel.

8. She is intellectual and well-cultured.

9. She achieves balance by being successful in all her roles.

10. She knows her worth and does not settle for less.

11. This woman will train others how to respect her and how to treat her by the way she respects and treats herself.

12. Her beauty together with her intelligence and spirituality equals Desirability.

13. She is the missing part of a man's ribcage.

14. She is not just beautiful on the outside, she is beautiful within.

15. Her life is a garden, and she a gardener.

7
Your Husband, Your King

*I*n the beginning God created the earth and the heavens. He then formed man from the dust of the ground. He planted a garden and a river to water the garden. After God had created everything, he looked at man, and for the first time he said it is not good. "It is not good that the man should be alone, I will make him a helper as his partner," he said. It was then that God formed every animal and bird and brought them to the man for him to name them and find a suitable helper as his partner. There was not found a helper as his partner for the man among the animals and the birds. So God caused a sleep to fall on the man and as he slept, he took one of his ribs and closed it with flesh. Out of Adam's rib God made the first woman and brought her to him. Her name was Eve which means "giver of life." Just as it was for Adam and Eve, so will it be for you and your husband one day. God has already made you out of a man and knows that it is not good for him to be alone. At the right moment, He will bring his helper who is you to him. When God brings you to that man he will be all that you have desired. You my dear will be the part of him that has been missing. You will be a giver of life to him. You will have a very valuable place in his life and on this earth. It will be totally awesome, so get ready to give a man life and treat him like what he will be, "your husband, and your king.

The Infamous "List"

I don't know what your experience with the "list" is. I have heard mixed reviews on it. Some people like it, some people don't. Some people have one and after a while give up on the list. I don't care what people say about it, I have one, oh and by the way, it's specific, very specific. I have close to 100 things on it, that's okay though, because the God I know wants to give me not just some things, but all things, and the desires of my heart.

So does having a list make me picky? My friends think I am. That is my friends that are still in the world. They tell me that I am never going to meet the right man, because I want too much. It's funny they tell me I'm going to get to heaven and ask God why he didn't send me a husband and God is going to look at me like I am crazy and tell me "what are you talking about, I sent you so and so, and so and so, and so and so!" This reminds me of a funny story that was sent to me via email. It went something like this: a man is perishing in a flood, he's holding on to a piece of wood, and he just knows the Lord is going to save him, a helicopter comes by and offers to save him and he says "No thanks, I am waiting on the Lord to save me", a boat comes by and offers to save him and he says "No thanks, I am waiting on the Lord to save me" well he drowns, he gets to heaven and ask the Lord, "Lord what happened? I was waiting on you to save me", the Lord replies, "I sent the helicopter, I sent the boat and you wouldn't let them save you!"

So back to the question, am I picky? Not! I just know what I am worth, and what I deserve. I won't settle for anything less and have no doubt in my mind that my God in heaven loves me so much, that he will give me all I want. Most importantly, I don't ask for anything I can not be or do myself.

May he grant you your heart's desire, and fulfill all your plans.
Psalm 20:4

Now about my list, I have broken it down, to be as specific as possible, so let me give you an idea. I have the "absolute essentials"; those are the things I will not compromise. For example, first on my list is that he has to be a "Christian" I mean a Christian who is on fire for God. On my list I have what I call "non-essentials" these are the things I am willing to compromise, for example doesn't have to have lots of money but have a decent job. Of course I have "the physical" for example; "tall, dark & handsome" you know the type, either George Clooney or JFK Jr. Okay, now I know we have covered this and realized that looks are not the most important thing, but they are important, I mean just as a woman needs to look good for a man, so does a man, need to look good for a woman. Next on my list, I have "please, please" for example "is creative, romantic." I also have on my list "absolutely not" for example cannot be "loud, obnoxious, arrogant." Next, there is the "personality." This one is very close to being essential. Something I have listed here is "outgoing." Next there's "really rather not" here I have listed, someone who watches too much television. I must admit that I have been so specific about my list that I even have "if I could have it all." For example, "Lord, let him have a masculine, deep, voice, kind of like Barry White and let him use it to sing to me.

Okay, remember what I said was the first thing on my list, which by the way should be the first thing on your list. Is that the man is a Christian. I mean he needs to be completely sold out to God. By that I don't mean that he calls himself a Christian and goes to church. I mean he has to pray, serve, know the word, live by the word and have a relationship with the Lord. Second, on your list is that the man has character and integrity. What I'm talking about here is a man of his word. You want him to say what he means and mean what he says. If the man says he's going to call you, by gosh he's going to call you. You want him to do the right thing even when no one is watching. I tell you in my life, I've met all kinds of men out there. Now the one that has a heart after God, now that's a king. Have no doubt that if a man is not sold out for God, he will not, that's right, he will not love you the way you want to be loved. Honestly, there is no more attractive quality, than a man who is sold out to God. I don't care how fine the brother is, how much money he has or what he does. You want a man who has God in him, because a man who has God in him will have all the good qualities of Him. He will love, he will serve, he will hate sin and he will be humble. Why else would you want a man who is sold out to God? I'll tell you why you want this man. A man that is sold out to God will not want to hurt God; therefore he will never hurt you.

What else could you want? Huh? Girlfriend, there are some other things you should consider and want. You should want a man that will uplift and encourage you. A man who will complement who you are and what you do, you want a man who will meet your needs and reflects your passion and goals. Some other things, that are important. Family, oh please don't overlook the family. You need to know about his family. Granted there are exceptions to every rule, but there's always a possibility that the man will be a norm, that means he will turn out to be like his father. Find out about his father, how is he? How does his father treat his wife? What kind of relationship does he have with the family? How does he treat his mother? Girlfriend, you want a man who treats his mother, good, I am not kidding here. I think many women want to overlook this; the truth of the matter is that if he doesn't treat the woman who gave him life good, I don't care how good you think he treats you, in the end he will turn out to be no good.

I know from my own personal experience that God used the relationship the man in my life had with his mother to show me a thing or two. Let me tell you as soon as that woman came into our lives; I began to see him in a different light. His mother was a slave to him. I mean she did everything for him, took care of his kids, cooked for him, cleaned his house, and washed his clothes. I never noticed him do anything special for her. He didn't even take her out for Mother's Day. One day it really hit me; we were going to the store, and "mom" asked him for some cigarettes. He went to the store and did some shopping for himself, then got her cigarettes. When he got them he paid for them with the $20 she gave him, so that he could give her change back. Imagine that he wouldn't even spend $2 on his mom. Now at first I thought, well he doesn't want to get her cigarettes because they are bad for her health. I guess you can say I was trying to overlook it, but forget that he did get them. I had always known this guy to be tight with his money. I mean as tight as tight can be, however, I always thought that one day when I became his wife he would change, that is until I saw how he treated his mother. My advice to you if you see some treatment that's not to your liking or something not right. Let him know you have a problem that he's got to fix before you have something to do with him. I mean think about it, there might be a day when you might do something that might remind him of his mother, and then what?

There's an old song by one of my favorite group TLC that went something like "*what about your friends*"? Let's talk about friends. They are very important, and a man needs to have friends that have been around for a while. Let me get into what I mean about this. I would really be a little skeptical if a man didn't have even one old friend he could name. Now I know sometimes a man, especially a saved man who wasn't always saved might not want anything to do with old friends. That's understandable, but he should at least have some kind of contact. I started a whole new circle of friends when I became saved. I mean, I was no longer that girl that I once was. Out with the old, in with the new. I now had friends that shared with me the biggest part of my life. My "girls" that went back 18 and 20 years they were not out of the picture, let me tell you about those "girls", we had been through some stuff. Good and bad, and some ups and downs. We had our falling outs, but in the end we came out friends. Why? Because our friendship was worth it because, I had made an investment. I couldn't just walk away.

Face it, real friendships need to be worked on, they don't just happen. You are bound to have differences of opinions and falling outs, but you work through them, you don't quit, you don't just walk out. I guess what I am trying to say here is that if "he" has no friends, you should probably look at that as a red flag. Think about it, maybe he's not into really working things out, maybe when the going gets tough, he walks out. Now come on girlfriend, is that really the kind of man you want? I don't think so. Think about his friends, and if he has none, don't automatically think its okay.

All right, that's enough about my list, back to what you should do with your list. It's very important that you share your list with someone, a good friend, a girlfriend. Let me tell you why. That friend, when she knows your list will see past the looks and the romance, she will remind you of what you like and don't like. Believe me sometimes you will have a friend who is real and lets you have it. For instance, you might completely overlook the fact that he treats his mother like dudu, that's when your girlfriend will step in and remind you, "Remember you want a man who treats his mother good" "Did you not hear how bad he talked about his mother?" Do you understand what I'm saying? Okay, one more thing, please do not share specifically what's on your list with the man that is in your life, because, guess what? If you do, it will be a matter of time until he becomes your list, and you don't want that. You my dear want the man who is what's on your list to find you and when he does you want him to be real. You do not want a man that you have to turn into the man that's on your list. Know this if he isn't it, he will not become it.

God will either bring the right man to you, or change some of the things you think you want. Please one more thing, don't stick to the list without being willing to make adjustments, you must be willing to compromise. I promise you sometimes compromise is worth it. Don't restrict God by having him stick to the list. I mean, I knew a girl who would not compromise at all, of all things she had on her list, she had that the man had to dance. Can you believe that, he had to dance? She was not going to compromise on that at all, when I asked her about it, she would say, "I love to dance and he better dance and that's it"! Now come on, being of Puerto Rican decent, and having that Latin rhythm in me, I love to dance. I guess you can say it's in my blood, I mean I was quite the dancer in "my worldly" days. I was all about Salsa, Merengue and had to have a man that danced. That's one of the things I loved the most about the man that was in my life for so long. As a matter of fact, we reunited on the dance floor. How times have changed. If the man in my life now was everything but a dancer, I wouldn't care about that, I'll teach him how to dance myself. He doesn't have to come to me knowing how. I know what I said about not changing a man, but you can certainly add some rhythm to him. God would not mind that at all.

Believe me, somehow or another you will be found by a man who's all the important things on your list. It might even be that God surprises you.

The man God provides for you might turn out to be some things you love, that weren't even on your list. You might find yourself compromising on the things you thought were important to you. I remember learning that lesson too well. I had met someone, who became so special to me and he, was so different than what I had on my list. He was much younger than I was, and he had kids from different women. After my last relationship with a man who had kids with different women and what I went through with those women, that was something I definitely did not want to have to deal with. Also, he had a job, not a career and he had not gone to college, nor was he financially stable. Well guess what, I didn't care about any of those things. This man was so much the essentials on my list that it made up for what he wasn't. It got to a point where I didn't even care about that list anymore. I remember that when we decided our relationship would just be a friendship, which was not quite what I would have wanted it to be, I was totally okay with it. I was okay with it because I knew God knew what he was doing, and realized that maybe he was holding out on bringing me the man that was everything on my list, or turning this man into it. First, he wanted to teach me one of the best lessons I would ever learn. Believe me I learned that you cannot stick to a list. If you do, you will limit God and my dear that is something you do not want to do. Think about it. Has it ever happened to you that you thought you wanted something and in the end wanted something else? I know I have.

I'd like to share with you an interesting story and how the Lord used mulch of all things to show me how there are things better out there than the things we think we want. Yes I'm talking about dirt. Goes to show how the Lord can use everything. I was working on the yard one day and went to buy mulch. Well, I preferred Red Shredded Mulch. That's the kind I had always used, I paid for the bags, and then went behind the store to have it loaded in my trunk. Well guess what? When I showed my receipt they loaded the mulch, the wrong mulch. They loaded Pine Bark Mulch, I tell the guy "That's not the mulch I wanted, I want Red Schredded Mulch." Well the guy tells me that I have to go inside the store because that's the mulch I paid for, and I had to make the adjustment, when I saw the line inside, I thought "forget it, I don't have time for this." I ended up taking the Pine Bark Mulch. I went home and mulched my yard, and to my disbelief, I loved this mulch. It made my yard look better than ever. Better than it would have if things had been my way. I remember this day looking up to heaven and telling God, "Alright Lord, you are trying to teach me something, I get it!" "I'll trust you for you always have something better for me than what I want myself."

Is He the One?

If you are anything like me you have probably met many men and wondered "Is He the One?" I have wondered the answer to this question countless times. You have probably thrown the question out there. Maybe you have pulled flower petals, doing the "he loves me, he loves me not" thing. I know I have. I mean I didn't always know God so why did I need to ask him? Now that I know God and have a relationship with Jesus I ask the question of him because I want to hear from him "he's the one." Don't you? Be real as women we need confirmation from God. Sadly enough some women hear what they want to hear and they make poor choices, they marry a man, divorce him and then blame it on God. Honey, God does not work like that, He gives you the choice to have a choice he, doesn't make the choice for you. What I think happens is that if we don't think the answer will be what we want it to be, we don't even ask. You've heard it, "ask and you shall receive." Sometimes what we receive is not what we want to receive. So it is with God's answer to the question "Is he the One" we don't want to hear "he's not the one," so we don't ask. I am here to tell you that you need to be prepared for God's answer no matter what it is.

Obviously I have not yet heard from God: "he's the one," after all I am still single. I do remember though the first time I heard God's voice, his words were "he's not the one." I had not even asked him the question, I had not because, I knew he wasn't the one, and did not want confirmation.

So what happens when we do not hear God's voice? How can we tell if "he's the one?" Let me give you some pointers. It's all about what the man is made of. We have already covered many things. Remember the things on the list. He should be in your family, by that I mean he should be a Christian. He should be completely sold out to God. He needs to have character, and integrity. "So what else?" You might be thinking. I am here to tell you some more nitty-gritty stuff about this man. He needs to be concerned about your well-being and provision. I love the story in the bible about Jacob and how he worked for seven years to win Rachel's heart, think about it. The man that is for you will work to win your heart. Not only that but he will work to provide for you. He will work to give you a good life, a good home and a life that is comfortable. I tell you the man that is for you would not want it any other way. This man will want a palace for you to live in and luxury for you to lavish in. This man will not feel like a real man until he's provided this for you and it ain't anything about pride. It's about a desire that is built within him to treat you like royalty. So honey, if a man is living off you or if he is not enhancing your surroundings, making a good life for you, then maybe he is not the one. Now come on I am not making material things the big deal here. I am just saying that just like Jacob, a man does have to work to win the prize that is you. I mean if he's not even trying, then there's a problem.

Let me tell you something, I bought a beautiful home all on my own, I mean beautiful. Any man would be made to feel like he didn't have to work. To be honest it scared me, at first. I mean I thought a man would either be intimidated thinking I was too much to take care of or worst, a man would be interested because he would not have to do much, I mean I practically lived like a queen on my own. Then I learned my worth and what I deserved. I learned about the man that God had for me. I learned that he would want to add to what I already had, that there was still work for him to do. This man would build me a pool or a garden or want to provide for me so that I could stay at home and enjoy what I had worked so hard to attain. He was not going to just move in and reap the fruits of my labor. He was not just going to enjoy what I had. Oh no he was going to want to make my life even better.

So what else about this man will show you that "he's the one?" Let me keep going. This man will want to protect you. He will want to know your whereabouts and business at all times, not because he's controlling but because he genuinely cares and want to know you are okay. This man will also want to make you feel secure. I mean this in the sense that you know he has your best interest at heart. You know he will take care of whatever needs to be taken care of. I mean this in the sense that he will never give you a reason to be jealous or fear infidelity on his part because he will not have a roaming eye. He will not flirt, and he will always give you your place.

What else? Let's not forget of course about love. We will get into this in depth in a future chapter. For now do know that you must have the God kind of love, the kind of love that is expressed in the "love chapter." That's the kind of love the man that God has for you will have. 1 Corinthians 13 if you don't know it, read it, and read it, and read it till it sinks in, and if the man you think is for you does not show you that kind of love then he doesn't love you. Remember the man God has for you will be the physical manifestation of your Lord, so he will love you exactly the way the Lord loves you.

Husbands love your wives, just as Christ loved the church and Gave himself up for her.
Ephesians 5:25

In the same way, husbands should love their wives as they do Their own bodies. He who loves his wife loves himself. For no one ever hates his own body, but he nourishes and tenderly cares for it, just as Christ does for the church.
Ephesians 5:28-29

Okay this is important, especially for women who have been on their own for a while and are so use to being in charge. Please, please, please ladies, when the man God has for you comes into your life, let go and let him be in charge, submit to his headship. Allow him to sweep you off your feet and be the man God wants him to be. I sincerely believe that sometimes-strong women can hold men back. Don't make that grave mistake, if you want a man, my gosh let him be a man.

> *Wives be subject to your husbands as you are to the Lord. For the Husband is the head of the wife just as Christ is head of the church, The body of which he is the Savior. Just as the church is subject to Christ, so also wives ought to be in everything to their husbands.*
> *Ephesians 5:22-24*

The Missing Rib

As a wife you are to be by your husband's side. To be by his side is why you were made from his rib. You will fit perfectly in his rib cage to protect his most vital organs. You are neither from his head to be above him or from his feet to be trampled by him. Oh no, you are from his side to be equal to him and to stand by him. It is your duty as the missing rib is to support and respect him and to protect him by not betraying his trust, or sharing his secrets, and by not discussing his weaknesses. A wife never speaks negatively of her husband, either in public or in private. She stands by him through right and wrong. She will guard his heart and if necessary she will condemn his wrong but never, ever condemn him.

When you are finally with your future husband:
1. Both of you will see the pieces of the puzzle fit together.
2. Your husband will see that you are the helper that he was waiting on to complete him, and totally fall in love with you.
3. You will see that the things that took place in your life were so the Lord could be glorified through your marriage.

So the Lord God caused a deep sleep to fall upon the man, and he slept; then he Took one of his ribs and closed up its place with flesh. And the rib that the Lord God had taken from the man he made into a woman and brought her to the man.
Then the man said,
"This at last is bone of my bones and flesh of my flesh; this one shall be called Woman, for out of Man this one was taken.

Genesis 2:21-23

Know that you were created from some man's rib therefore; somewhere out there a man is missing a piece of himself. One day he will find you and when he does, he will know that you are perfect fit.

All Sales Final

If you are a lady, I know you know how to shop and I am sure you have bought "All sales final" or clearance items. You know that most of the time these items are marked "as is." Usually items marked "as is" have some kind of flaw. Most of the times you can see these flaws, but you buy it anyway. Sometimes there are flaws you don't even see. Anybody know what I am talking about?

It's pretty easy for us to buy a shirt, a blouse, a pair of jeans as is, sometimes we think "I'll fix it" right? We have a hard time though accepting a man "as is." We should know that what we see is what we get and we can't fix him. So many times we fool ourselves into thinking that we will choose this "as is" man and we or he will change his flaws. Once we get married, forget about it. It ain't going to happen. A woman cannot change a man. Have you not learned that yet? You need to instead learn to enjoy each other while at the same time respecting and celebrating each other's differences without changing each other.

It is very important that you remember that the man God provides for you, you will have to accept "as is." In God's style of things, all sales are final that means if you marry the man. He provides for you "as is," you better accept him. You don't return, you don't exchange and you certainly don't make alterations to a human being. Only God can change and alter a man through our prayer and patience. So make sure you look real good before you buy. Don't even think about altering or changing this man. Instead of trying to change your husband, think about inspiring him and challenging him to rise up to all God has destined for him to be. I tell you with you by his side he will be a success. I promise you most successful men in the world had to work and climb a ladder to get to where they are. Most of the time with a woman in tow. Men do not always become successful on their own. If they do they won't be happy because they have no one to share their success with.

Think about the movie "Waiting to Exhale." I am sure most of you have seen that "chick flic". Remember, Angela Bissett's role. She stood by her man; he was nothing in the beginning, and then when he became all that with her help, he preferred another woman. Yes he left her, but she was left with that gorgeous "to die for" home, cars, money, lots of it and the kids. I'd say she reaped some benefit and think about it, he wasn't even a Godly man. How much more would a woman who marries a Godly man reap. I tell you there is no price you could put on it, because you will reap big, waaaaay big. Remember it's very likely that the man you marry will not turn out to be everything you wanted. He might even turn out to be damaged merchandise, but you chose him so you better accept him "as is."

Speaking of "as is" remember that old song that went something like "don't go changing, I love you just the way you are." Don't you go changing for someone, remember there is a man out there who you will be a perfect fit for and who will accept you "as is" and love you just the way you are.

Marry in the Family

The bible clearly discourages marrying nonbelievers. Now why would that be, after all doesn't the bible also tell us we are to love everyone and we are not to judge? That's right God want us to love everyone and to not judge, but he doesn't want us to marry someone who is not equally yoked to us. Meaning, he does not want us with someone who does not believe. Why? Let me tell you. God wants the foundation of your love and marriage to be the simple fact, that you share him. He knows that doing it any other way would not work. I remember boldly stating that I would not marry a man who was not a Christian. My friends, the ones that were not believers would ask me "what if you meet the perfect man but he wasn't Christian?" I would tell them "then he's not perfect." I mean come on if I couldn't share with him the biggest part of my life, what would we have?" How would it be going to church by myself and not feeling like I was able to talk to him about the message? How would it feel to not be able to stand in agreement with him in prayer? Now to the next question I was asked, "Well what if he started believing in God?" I would reply "Well he'd have to start believing in God and acting like it before we got together." I mean come on, I for one have witnessed guys who started going to church to win the heart of a Christian woman, knowing she is a "good catch," he deceives her, they marry, and then there she is at church by herself. You get the picture don't you? Last question, "Well, what if you could change him?" Not!!! I already touched on this, remember, as much as we'd like to believe we can change a man, we can't do it, nor is it our job to. It's God's job. Not only does a man have to believe, oh no he has to be a Christian in every sense of the word. Remember what I mean by that—he has to have a personal relationship with the Lord.

When it comes to choosing your lifetime companion, girlfriend, as a Christian you must choose to marry in the family. If you know what I mean. Let me tell you what I mean, I am not crazy. Ladies, what I am saying here is that a man must first be your brother, your brother in Christ that is. The man you marry should share your foundation, your faith and your values, just as you share with your siblings. You must marry someone who believes the things you believe in and understands your relationship with the Lord. You need to be able to talk to him about the biggest part of your life and grow together in God. No doubt about it, if you don't share the Lord, you will always be challenged and never agree. If you do, when problems arise and things go wrong and they will, together you will seek answers from the same source and stand on the same promises. Think about it. A house divided cannot stand. Neither can a marriage if the partners are not made of the same material, of the same standards. After all, how could two resolve a problem when one thinks there is no problem?

Best Friends

Your marriage should be based on a friendship. In fact, you should marry your best friend. Best friends have a friendship that is so strong that in spite of the worst circumstances, a betrayal for instance at the end the person you want to talk with, and share what it is you are feeling is your friend, your best friend, the person you are married to.

It is a strong friendship that will make a marriage work and worth fighting for. Everything else that exists between a man and a woman outside of friendship, I'm talking about attraction, lust, sex, memories it will not be enough to last a lifetime. I know this from personal experience. As friends, you each have a part of you invested in each other that no one can easily replace, therefore, you are more willing to fight against anything that comes your way in order to not lose a part of you.

You have no idea how strong a marriage can be when you are each other's absolute best friend. Imagine you want to share everything with each other. The good, the bad, the happy and the sad. You'll have each other to celebrate with, mourn with. You will have each other to find physical comfort in. Being best friends, as well as husband and wife is incredibly powerful, nothing compares to it.

His speech is most sweet and he is altogether desirable. This is my Beloved and this is my friend, O daughters of Jerusalem.
Song of Soloman 5:16
As husband and wife you need to not only love each other as such, but also love each other as friends. Friends

that know each other better than anyone else could know you. I am talking about the nitty-gritty here. Everything there is to know. You need to know each other's likes and dislikes, turn-ons and turn-offs, quirks and pet peeves, strengths and weaknesses, successes and failures, gifts and talents, character flaws, good qualities and bad qualities, hopes and dreams. You need to be able to know each other's feelings about family, finances, sex, children, and friends. There should be no secrets between you or information hidden from one another. You share everything, no matter what it is. No man out there should be carrying more about you than your husband. No woman should be carrying more about your husband than you. Know each other like you know yourself and be each other's best friend.

Stand by your Man

Understand that you were designed for the man that God brings to you. With the position of "wife" there exist many duties you must honor. First and foremost, you must honor and respect your husband. A duty you have as a wife is to "stand by your man", remember you are made from his side to protect him, to honor him, to respect him, and to submit to him, that means you stand by him.

As a wife it is your duty to make your husband look good and have a good reputation. Don't let anyone make you think you are a small thing. For you my dear have the ability to affect everything that is vital to your husband. It is said that behind every good man is a good woman. Why do you think? Let me tell why girlfriend, the presence of a woman in a man's life makes a man grounded. Think about it, when a man has his stuff together at home, he is more dedicated to succeed in everything he does. This is so true that sometimes when being considered for a position, for a partnership, for membership, a man's wife is examined, sometimes even more so than he is. That's why you hear stories about men messing around with the wrong type of women, telling them they love them, but never leave their wives for them. I bet these "wives" are "miss goody two shoes" which by the way is a good thing, so don't get offended. These women make their men look good.

An important way you stand by your man is by allowing him to trust you. Trust is one of the most essential ingredients in the marriage relationship. Imagine not having trust. How would a husband and wife fulfill their individual divine purposes if they spent their time constantly worried about each other's whereabouts, worrying if they are being faithful, if they are being honest, if they will betray them or if they are going to stab each other in the back?

Only with a strong foundation of trust in God and each other can you build a life and know that if a storm comes it won't be easily blown away. Only with trust in place will your man know that you will stand by him.

Sweetness on Your Lips

Then God said, "let there be light"; and there was light.
Genesis 1:3

It is amazing how God created the earth with the mere power of his words. Just as amazing is the fact that as a woman, you have incredible power with your words, so much power that through them you can influence a man more than anything else can. Think about it: throughout his life it was a feminine that disciplined him, scolded him, encouraged him, soothed him, advised him, often taught him and prayed with him.

Pleeeese ladies, Pleeeese, one thing that you must do is watch your words, for the bible teaches us that life and death is in the tongue. Knowing this, be careful with what your tongue speaks and don't abuse your power. Your words spoken sweetly and gently can make a man move. Your words are to be constructive, in other words they need to exalt your man, build him up, uplift him, and if your words are destructive they will tear him down. At times even make him feel like a failure, like he's impotent, girl that is no good.

Let no evil come out of your mouths, but only what is useful For building up as there is need, so that your words will give Grace to those who hear.
Ephesians 4:26

Know this and never forget it. For every negative word you say to your husband, there is a pretty young thing out there wanting to share the sweetness on her lips with him and whisper sweet things in his ears. Don't give her a chance. Don't let your words destroy what you have. I know it seems simple and small, but words are really gigantic. If used negatively they can start wars, divide countries, destroy relationships, incriminate the innocent, damage opportunities, hurt children, scar women, and intimidate men. The saddest things about words, is that once they are said, that's it, they cannot be erased, or be retracted.

A cheerful heart is a good medicine, but a downcast spirit dries up the bones.
Proverbs 17:22
Have sweetness on your lips when you speak to your husband. When he hears your voice he will feel respected

and honored in such a way it will stir up excitement and passion. Speak to him in a way that he will never feel pain. Talk to him in a way that he will love to call you often, just to hear your sweet voice. He will want to race home. Say something to him that when he hangs up he will be happy he called. Do not ever speak to your husband in a way that when he hangs up that he'll say, "Why did I call her for anyway?" Don't speak to your husband in a way that he does not want to come home. Let me tell you after a while that will start to hurt and he will look elsewhere for sweet words. Believe me, you do not want that. Instead you want a man who races home to hear soothing, positive words. If you say words that bring him down you will drive him away to an addiction, work holism or into the arms of another. Remember one more thing, it is not enough that you just talk good to your husband; you have to talk good about your husband. This is so important because a husband will thrive on the validation he gets from his wife. Have sweetness on your lips when your words have anything to do with him, when you talk to him and when you talk about him.

Remember that a man falls in love with a woman because of how she makes him feel. Believe me the hurt from words is not something that is easily healed. The pain lasts for a long time, sometimes longer than the person who caused it is around. I have been a victim of abuse, both physical and emotional. I am here to tell you that the words that were said to me hurt more than the fractured arm, broken nose, bruised ribs. The "I am sorry" no matter how many times, were never enough to make the hurt heal. Being spoken to the way I was made me feel so low, like I was worth nothing. It's a feeling I would never want to cause my husband to feel, neither should you. There is power in your words, do not abuse the power, and always have sweetness on your lips.

Anxiety weighs down the human heart, but a good word cheers it up.

Proverbs 12:25

Qualified for the Position

You wouldn't apply for a position without first knowing the job description and requirements to ensure you are qualified for the position would you? Sadly enough there are many women who apply for the position of wife without understanding the job description and requirements before they apply. They are made an offer and anxiously and excitedly accept. They start on the job, and then guess what? They don't last long. Why do you think? Could it be that maybe, there is so much more required for this position than just being a woman?

Examine yourselves, and only then eat of the bread and drink of the cup.

1 Corinthians 7:28

Believe me when I tell you, that not every woman qualifies for the position of a wife. Maybe that is why the word says that he who finds a wife finds a good thing. It doesn't say he who finds a woman finds a good thing. Does it? So why do you think it's so specific about the word wife? Could it be that it is easy to find a woman? A wife though, one that lets her husband be the head of her is not?

But I want you to understand that Christ is the head of every man, and the husband is the head of his wife, and God is the head of Christ.

1 Corinthians 11:3

I don't know about you but that tells me that maybe I need to be acting like a wife before he comes around. Now my dear friend, that does not mean you just assume a role that has not given to you I mean, don't start doing his laundry and cooking for him, but do the other things. Encourage him, support him, partner with him, and be his friend. Being a wife is the most important position you will ever hold, even more so than that of a mother. What? You didn't know you are a good mother. When in the position you are first a good wife. Being a wife is a position that is life-consuming. It is by all means more than an 8-5 job and you better know what the expectations of you will be before you accept the offer.

Ladies do not be disheartened; you do not need previous experience to qualify for this position. I have seen many women qualify for the position without any experience. Now if you happen to have some, remember what you learned when you previously held the position, it might come in handy. So how do these ladies do it you might ask? It's simple they allow the Holy Spirit to teach them. They get into the word and learn, read books that help them, and they ask questions to women who have proven themselves to be successful at the position.

All right then, you know what you need to do, so get to it. When the position becomes available, you can apply and the man that is seeking for the position to be filled will see that you my dear are qualified.

The Purpose of Marriage

Marriage is one of the greatest gifts God gave us. One that should not be accepted lightly. Marriage is a union that needs to be held in honor, as something that is cherished, esteemed and worthy. Marriage is above all things about love. Therefore, it is to personify God. God ordained marriage, and designed it to bring glory to him and to exemplify him and his love. One of the greatest things about marriage is that it is the physical manifestation of the type of relationship God wants to have with us.

> *So, we have known and believe, the love God has for us. God is love And those who abide in love abide in God and God abides in them.*
> *1 John 4:16*

God intends for marriage to be a lot more than meeting, feeling attracted, dating, courting, falling in love and joining in holy matrimony. It is the coming together of two to be more effective for him. It's about displaying kingdom living and expanding his kingdom by the example of your living together. On the other hand marriage is by no means just the coming together of a man and woman and glorifying God. It is the crashing of two lives, two sets of histories, backgrounds, childhoods, cultures, customs, memories, experiences, habits, beliefs and values. In spite of all its differences, issues, conflicts and challenges, marriage is a sacred, beautiful thing. It is a covenant relationship, by that I mean a permanent commitment that lasts a lifetime and requires constant maintenance and nurturing. For the sake of the covenant, when you make a decision to marry, you have to understand and have the mindset that the decision you make will be forever. There is no "well if it doesn't work, we can always get divorced." Oh no! When making this decision, which is the most important decision of your life, after accepting the Lord, you should first be able to see yourself with this person for the rest of your life. Then you should pray and pray and have God show you if this is the person you are to be with forever. Think about it, can you honestly tell your husband "I want to grow old with you!" If you can't answer yes to this question stop before you do something crazy. Make sure you know what you are doing. One day you will stand before God, your pastor, your friends and family and in a few minutes make vows you will have to honor for forty, fifty or even more years. Know this, for richer, for poorer, for better, for worst, in sickness and in health, every part of it will come to pass. Make sure you understand, and when you say "I Do," you mean "I Do."

When that day comes you will stand next to your future husband and you will be joined in Holy Matrimony. At that moment you and he will see the pieces of the puzzle fit together. You will see that the things that took place in your lives were so the Lord could fulfill His purpose for Him to be glorified through your marriage.

Final Word

Marriage is a wonderful thing, with that being said; I must say I enjoyed writing this chapter almost as much as I enjoyed writing the previous chapter on being a woman. I know we women are hard to understand, there are even jokes about the subject, but let's face it men, they are no piece of cake. We need to get to know them. I hope you have found it exciting to learn about men and what they want and seek in a woman. I love to share things I have learned. I know it will help me be the kind of wife the Lord wants me to be and things that will help my marriage be successful. I for one want to put the things I have learned into practice with the special man who is in my life. I want to submit to him, respect him, honor him and without assuming a role that has not yet been given to me, act as a wife. Even if he turns out to not be my husband, I can get training and be qualified in the future when the position becomes available and it is offered to me. Once in the position, I want to blow away my boss (God) by conducting myself excellently. It is my deepest and sincere wish that your heart, eyes and mind have been opened. It is also my sincere desire that you have seen just how important you will be to the man God has for you and what it takes to be a good wife. That you will appreciate marriage for it is God's greatest gift and once married you and your husband will live out the purpose for your marriage. Most importantly, think of that special man God has for you will be "Your Husband, Your King."

Prayer

Father God, I thank you for the wonderful man, you have brought into my life for me to share my walk with you and my life with. Thank you, Lord for ordering his steps to find me and to see me as his missing rib.   I thank you Lord for granting the desires of my heart. For he is, more than I could ever want. I thank you, because you have chosen him to be my best friend, my leader, my head, my covering and my husband. Lord, teach me to accept him just as he is and never try to change him or judge him. Thank you, Lord for preparing me to be his helper, confidant, friend, companion, partner & supporter. Lord, I ask you to give me grace to use my tongue for your glory and to always speak sweetness and blessings over him. Lord, protect our marriage from anything that is not of you. Shield us from anyone who would have evil plans and desires for us. Lord, I ask that you equip us with the desire to serve each other. Keep away anything that would threaten us in any way, especially things like drugs, alcohol, lust, temptation, pornography, gambling, lying deceit, infidelity, obsession, and negative words. Always, be the foundation of our relationship. Let there never be thought of divorce in either one of our hearts or minds. Lord, help us to always make time for each other. Unite us in a way that our love and trust grows stronger day by day and glorifies you in every way. Lord, help me be a blessing to my husband in every way, in Jesus' Name. Amen.

Tips on Making Your Husband, Your King

Pray for him

Make sure he always comes home to a calm home.

Submit to him.

Encourage & uplift him, be his cheerleader.

Make him second only to God in your life.

Commit that you will always work things out. Never walkout or hang up.

Listen to him.

Respect him.

Make it safe for him to trust you.

Never assume, accuse or attack.

Guard your tongue when speaking to him.

Accept him with the bad, remember no one is perfect.

Never bring up something that was shared in confidence.

Provide the "woman" things, clean house, clean clothes, and good meal.

Say good morning, good night, sleep and wake up in each other's arms.

Make "making love" exciting and pleasing to him. Never have a headache.

Always look your best for him.

Surprise him with little things. E.g. notes, cards, candlelight dinner, flowers.

Continue to do what you did when he fell in love with you.

8
"What is Love?"

*L*ove can be a very splendored thing. It's something so wonderful that even when it appears as if it has forgotten us, we should never forget it. No doubt about it that the business of falling in love, loving and being loved is many times a gamble. A gamble that involves many, many risks is love in deed, yet in spite of the risks, more often than not we are very willing to take them and do not allow them to stop us from feeling such an incredible thing. Let's face it, love, is something that is much sought after and sometimes plunged right into even once having the knowledge it could result in a regrettable and painful experience. Why? Because every single one of us, was made to love and to be loved. There is much to be learned about love, it's one of those things like a class you have to take over and over again till you finally get the credit for it. Personally, after many years I am an "honors graduate" of the "it's better to have loved and lost than to have never loved at all" school. Had I learned about love early on, and what it costs to have my love, what schooling would I had saved myself from. Well, it's not too late; I learned what I did for a reason so here it goes, my teaching on "What is Love?"

Love, Plain & Simple

So what is this thing we call love? Let me try to make it Plain & Simple. Sadly, in today's society the word love is expressed so loosely and given so many meanings, it's no wonder it has ceased to mean what it should mean. Thank God, that he gave us the bible to teach us what it is. I'm sure you've read 1 Corinthians 13, the "Love Chapter", or at least heard it, for it is often used at weddings and I know you've gone to some weddings. Whether you have read it or heard it, chances are that even if you've never experienced love you must have an idea of what it should be.

Love is patient; love is kind; love is not envious or boastful or arrogant or rude. It does mot insist on its own way; it is not irritable or resentful; it does not rejoice in wrongdoing, but rejoices in the truth. It bears all things, believes all things, hopes all things, endures all things. Love never ends.
1 Corinthians 13:4-8

I challenge you to think of love, as what Corinthians describe it to be, in the "Love Chapter" and not what the world says it is.   In the world love can mean so many things that it was never intended to mean. I don't know about you but to me, it's sad to know that the same word that should stir up so much from the heart and be associated with a special person and our feelings for them is the same word that is sometimes associated with insignificant things such as seafood, sushi, and shopping ("I love seafood, sushi, shopping, etc.").   Please know that love has to do with passion, feelings, emotions and chemistry towards someone just as much at it does with the association of something positive.

What else is love? It is something that is given freely and unconditionally. You cannot force someone to love you, to do that would be to not really be loved, for a person must be able to choose to love, if they have no free will to choose, they might not really love you. It is for that reason that what God wants most from us is love, something that he cannot force us give and comes from our own free will.

> *For God so loved the world that he gave his only Son, so that everyone who believes in him may have eternal life.*
>
> *John 3:16*

It's amazing, how sometimes simply by knowing what things are we know what they are not. Talk about plain and simple; it does not get plainer or simpler than that. With that said wouldn't it be safe to say that by knowing the love that the Corinthians described in the "Love Chapter" you can pretty much know what it is not?

So what else is there to know about love? How about this "love at first sight" thing? Well that's easy; let me tell you, love is not something that happens at first sight. That's right! Contrary to popular belief there is no such thing as "Love at First Sight", really, how could there be? There is no way love could be recognizable immediately. Seldomly is it even recognizable after just a few months. Sorry, but what you think is love at first sight is not, it's lust, big difference, we will be talking about that shortly. Love is something that only through time and after you have shared and overcome tough challenges and still end up together, is love.

Something else to know about love is that it is not a cure for pain, it's not like it happens and whalah, everything is okay. Ironically, it is love that so many times causes us pain.

Love Vs. Being in Love

I'm sure you've heard the saying, maybe it's been told to you. "I love you, but I'm not in love with you". Ohhhhh, that hurts. Some people can't figure it out, they wonder. "What do you mean, you love me but you're not in love with me"? Well I've never been quite there, but I felt that when things were not happening for me, the way I thought they would with my friend and I. Let me try to take a stab at explaining it to you, maybe it will make some sense.

There's a real fine line between loving someone and being in love with someone. I remember in regards to my "special friend", people would ask me how I felt, and I would tell them, "I love him very much, but I don't know if I'm in love with him, I mean, were really just friends. I don't know him yet at the level where I can say I'm in love with him". All along though, I felt like I was in love, I mean I became excited when he called, I looked especially nice when we were going to see each other, I thought about him and wanted to be with him all the time. I sure felt like I was in love, but really I couldn't say I was in love with him.

I don't know what it is about being in love with someone, but it makes you act differently then when you just love someone. There are things you do for someone you are in love with that you do not do for someone you just love. Like how about being romantic? I know that was one of the first things that changed when my relationship with my "special friend" went to the next level. We were romantic. Don't get me wrong you do things for someone you love, but you take things deeper when you are in love or at least think you are. Do you understand what I'm saying? When you are in love, you worship and revel the person you are in love with. You are very, very sweet. You seek to please that person by giving them what they want (except yourself). Ladies, your desire is to make that man feel special should be strong and second only to your love for God. Think about it, you know what I'm talking about, you know because you've done it.

When you love someone, you do just that, you love him or her. It is sad to see how once two people are in love with each other they change and begin to take things for granted. Many times after the love has been proclaimed both the man and the woman stop doing the things they did that made them fall in love with each other. Once two people are married, forget about it. Talk about two people changing; they don't even look the same anymore. It's no wonder that husbands and wives fall out of love with each other. How sad, huh? My own personal experience from observing men with women is that men…. especially stop doing the things that made the woman they are with fall in love with them. I believe that's why so many people say they love who they're with, but they are no longer in love with them. Sadly, many of us after we love someone and know that they love us back, change our ways. Ever heard, "once you are married keep doing the things you did when you fell in love"? How about, "when I first met him he use to….", or "when I first met her she use to…."? How heartbreaking. I tell you that those words are not said in vain. Whoever came up with that deserves a hand. I tell you the feelings you feel and the way you act should stay the same long after you proclaim your love for each other that way you both continue to fall in love even deeper.

If you are married and reading this book, please take heed to what I'm saying. Remind your husband everyday of what made him fall in love with you. Do not get to the point where you stop doing the things you use to do. I promise you, if you do the things that made him fall in love with you continuously, he will fall deeper and deeper in love with you with each passing day. Now, if your husband has stopped doing what made you fall in love with him, remind him so that he will go back to doing those things. I tell you the feelings you feel and the way you act should be the same long after you proclaim your love for each other. If they change they need to for the better. Understand that sometimes things will change, but you my dear don't have to change.

About the difference between loving someone and being in love with someone, think about the men in your own life. Think about when you were "in love" with them, now think about when you just loved them. There was a difference, wasn't there? We kind of took them for granted some, once we knew they loved us, huh? Now, seriously, think about the men you have fallen in love with. I dare to say men, because not many of us have fallen in love with just one man in our life. Right? Well except for my sister, she was married when she was 16, and about to celebrate a 20-year anniversary, Praise God.

So what was it about them that made you fall in love with them? I don't know about you, but for me, it was always how special they made me feel, the way they showed me they loved me and the wonderful things they did for me. Now close your eyes and think about God. Does he not make you feel more special than anyone else? Does he not love you more than anyone else ever has? How about this, has he not done more wonderful things for you than anyone has? I mean think about it, God's hands have been all over your life and doing things in it, probably since before you ever knew him, and there is still yet so much more he wants to do. So now that you know there's a difference between loving and being in love, apply what you have learned and don't just love the Lord, fall in love with Him.

Love Does Cost a Thing

One of the greatest divas in recent years, a Puerto Rican from Bronx, New York, like me, Jennifer Lopez sings a song titled *"Love Don't Cost a Thing"*. I don't mean to burst JLo's bubble, cause when she first came on the scene I loved her and what she did for us puerto rican women, but contrary to her song's title, love does cost a thing. I am of course talking about the love of a man costing something, not the love of God. God's love, now, that's a love that don't cost a thing. It's already ours. I will be sending poor JLo a copy of this book so she can learn about love and I can hopefully help my sista out.

So let's talk about a woman's love and what it should cost. Girl, your love should cost something, granted not diamonds and such things but something. Let's first understand this, there is a difference between cost and price. Cost is: *value measured by what must be given, done or undergone to obtain something*, while price is: *a predetermined price or amount of goods given in exchange for something else*. Let me give you an example, of something that has a price and something without price, yet both have a cost. Take for instance, an automobile has a price that is predetermined and much cost associated with it. There's the maintenance, gas, insurance and time involved taking care of all those things. Now, think about your salvation. There is no price you have to pay for your salvation, (it's already been paid) but it costs to be saved. There's the saying no to many things you use to say yes to, there's time that you have to put into your relationship with the Lord, there's the letting go of friendships and relationships that influence you in a negative way. Understand the difference between the two? See where I'm going?

You should never put a price on your love, for in doing so you will cheapen it and making it affordable, something you don't want to do for my dear, what you have to offer is priceless. Remember you are not a piece of merchandise or clothing that a guy can just try like a sample and he can discard when he feels he no longer has a need for you. Oh no honey, you especially don't give a man a chance to decide if you are worth the cost he must pay to have you. So what does it cost to have your love? What are you worth?

Owe no one anything except to love one another for the one who Loves another has fulfilled the law.
Romans 13:8

So you are probably thinking, "aren't we suppose to just love"? Yes, of course we are suppose to just love-- everyone, and love him or her unconditionally, but for a man and a woman to have that "special" love should cost something. Please understand a man should not have to pay for your love, but your love should cost him something. In other words there is no price associated with your love, but there is a cost associated with your love. Remember that you are fearfully and wonderfully made and though you have no price, there's a cost to have you. Is the man in your life willing to pay the cost? Let me give you a clue that he is. If the man you are with does not respect you, does not honor you, or encourage you, he my dear does not love you or deserve you and will not be willing to pay what it cost to have your love.

I love the bible story in Genesis where Jacob falls in love with Rachel. Talk about a guy who was willing to pay whatever the cost. Oh, and his attitude, wow, what woman would not want a man like that?

So Jacob served seven years for Rachel, and they seemed to him but a few days because of his love for her.
Genesis 29:20

I love this scripture because it means that Jacob loved Rachel so much that it didn't matter how much he had to work for her. That's how real love is, no matter what the cost is, it is not high enough; that man that says he loves you if he really loves you will be willing to do whatever he has to do to earn your love or pay it's cost. So don't sell yourself short, make sure you have a cost, do not negotiate it, do not lower it, if he's the one, I assure you, just like Jacob, he will pay whatever the cost.

The Difference Lust Makes

There is a big difference between someone who loves you and someone who lusts over you. We have got to talk about this. Lust is a very powerful thing, (and all the ladies said Amen!!!!) it's one of our enemy's favorite weapons and he likes to use it against us. I'm here to tell you that a man lusting over you is not what you want. You want a man who loves you and doesn't just lust over you. For a man to feel both, but for his love to be greater is a wonderful thing. I would want the man God has for me to lusts for me, but only after he loves me more. Believe me to lust more than to love is not a good thing.

Boy, do I know for I have been there and believe me that what I felt was not good. Please understand the difference and do not be fooled, for it would hurt to find out a man could make you feel so loved, when really what he is, is "in lust" with you. It's with great sadness that I share, I learned this lesson too well and it caused me much hurt. I couldn't tell at first but the man who had been in my life and who had made me feel so loved, the one I loved so much, really had been "in lust" with me. What hurt me most about this love was that at the end there was nothing left of the incredible love he had made me feel. All the wonderful things I once felt were gone, and in its place I felt a hatred from him I never would think I'd feel. I'm talking this man was so bitter and ugly to me, he would call the house to speak to my girls, and he couldn't be civil to me. We ran into each other at one of my daughter's sports event and he wouldn't even look at me. I use to pray that God would just touch his heart and soften it to the point he would be able to forgive, for deep down inside I wanted nothing but happiness for him, in spite of the fact that I couldn't give it to him. I knew our lives as we knew it to be was over, and we couldn't be friends, but to be civil to each other, was that really too much to ask for? It hurt me, and I beat myself up about it for a while. It hurt because regardless of all that had happened between us, all he had done to me and how he ripped my heart apart, I still loved him. Nothing could change that, because I really, sincerely from the bottom of my heart loved him. Maybe it wasn't what love should have been, but as much as I knew how to love, I loved him. Even when our love ended, deep inside of me, I still had love for him. I remember thinking "how could he love me so much and then hate me, maybe he never loved me at all"? It took me a while but it finally hit me and I accepted that he never really loved me. He lusted for me. His lust for me was so incredible that it had led him to believe that he loved me, therefore, he showed me love, and I of course concluded that he was in love with me. Well, as you already know things happen, and as he realized he could no longer have me, the love he had had for me turned to hate, a hatred that was even greater than the lust he had once.

The bible illustrates this lust turned to hate thing in the tragic story of Amon and Tamar found in 2 Samuel. In the story Amon, son of King David, "fell in love" with his beautiful half-sister Tamar and plotted to rape her. After he forced her to lay with him, he was seized with a loathing for her, that was greater then the lust he had felt for her and told her to "get out".

> *Then Amon was seized with a very great loathing for her; indeed, his loathing was greater than the lust he had felt for her.*
>
> *2 Samuel 13:15*

Letting Love Go

There's a popular saying that goes ways back; I remember as a teenager it hanging on a picture on my wall. It said *"If you love something set it free, if it comes back to you it was yours, if it doesn't, it never really was"*. Heard it? Now, I know to do this is hard. It's one of those easier said than done things right? One of those things that people can't bring themselves to do. I mean come on, no one wants to let go of something they love—especially when they know not for sure they will ever get it back. Letting go of something though, is a chance we sometimes have to take. Surprisingly, the Lord does something very special when we are willing to let go of something. It's like a reward for passing a test. I am reminded of the story in the bible of Abraham. Remember what happened when he was commanded to sacrifice his son Isaac as a burnt offering and was willing to let him go?

> *Then Abraham reached out his hand and took the knife to kill his son.*
> *But the angel of the Lord called to him from Heaven, and said*
> *"Abraham, Abraham!" and he said, "Here I am." He said, "Do not lay your hand on the boy or do anything to him; for now I know you fear God, since you have not withheld your son, your only son from me."*
> *Genesis 22:10-12*

I remember after feeling that "in love" feeling for almost a year and nothing happening, I decided it was time to take a chance on something happening or letting go of love. I took a chance on something happening by expressing my feelings and telling the man in my life, I loved him. Not only that, I also told him I believed in us and wanted us to have a future together. You must understand that this man and I were growing so close and spending so much time together, talking for hours every night, I felt we had a future and couldn't figure out his feelings. I guess you can say, I got to that point where I wanted to hear straight from the horse's mouth what was up. The point came, right around the holidays when I told myself "something has to give". We finally had a serious conversation that needless to say, did not go as I had anticipated. My "friend" told me he had thought about our lives together, but it was not in his heart to make a move. He told me that he did not want to restrict himself, and make a commitment to me when he wasn't 100% sure. In so many words he told me that there was no woman he was interested in, but in the event there was, he wanted the opportunity to get to know one.

Ouch!!!!! That hurt. So what? "Could he not be interested in me?" I wondered to myself. Here we were having all the characteristics of a boyfriend/girlfriend relationship. We loved each other and had a foundation already in place to have the best relationship, God was the center of our lives and we were best friends. I thought that's what you needed to have a great relationship. It made so much sense to me, why didn't it to him?

I had been patient for a year with this guy. My friends couldn't believe it, "Not you!", they said. I mean when I was in the world I was so use to having any man I wanted, I mean I liked a guy, and whalah, he was mine. Here was a man I truly loved like I had never loved before, and had been so attracted to and-nothing. This wonderful man, who I knew the Lord brought into my life to be my husband was unable and unwilling to see that we were brought together for a reason and it wasn't to be "just friends". He made it clear to me that he had not heard from God that I was the one and did not want to do anything because of it. I remember asking him a question: "You're waiting for God to tell you I'm the one. Has He told you I'm not the one? Cause you see He hasn't told me you're the one either, but, that's okay my heart has told me by the way it feels." "Is that not good enough for you"? I asked him, but he didn't say anything. Anyway, that day as we walked to our cars, we said good-bye after we told each other we loved each other and would always be in each other's lives. I told him I was going to miss him, for things were going to have to change. He asked me "When?" "When I get married?" I said "Oh no honey before that". "I mean our relationship is going to have to change--soon, especially if you think there could be another woman in your life in the future, after all, do you think you can call me late at night and we talk for hours if you have a girlfriend?" "I don't think so", I told him. I really think he never thought things would have to change, I mean he had had the best of both worlds for a while. Never before had I made it clear to him that our "friendship with privileges" would one-day end. Now let's get something straight those privileges were not physical—he had never even touched me in that way, hence what I said about being patient. I mean I'm into purity, but a nice romantic hug, a kiss, there's nothing wrong with that, I mean I'm strong, I could really deal with that. Anyway, so here I was a beautiful girlfriend he could call and talk to or spend time with whenever he wanted to. Well that day, as I drove back to work, in between the tears and calling myself dumb, I made an important decision. I decided that even though I did not want to lose what I had, I had to let love go. Well wouldn't you know I didn't have to? In just a matter of days my "friend" told me that he didn't know what he was thinking when he said the things he said and that he didn't want me to let go. He told me he wanted to pray about "us" and seek Godly counsel on our relationship. Praise God, I was willing to let him go, I really think that turned things around. Just six weeks later on Valentine's Day we took our relationship to the next level and one month later we were already talking about getting married, our vision for ministry and sharing our lives together.

To Love Again

You have just read about my wonderful love story, however it did not start that way. I must back track and share about where I was in my life before I met this amazing man.

Sadly, many of us at some point in our lives have loved so deeply and with all our heart, that when the love we feel ends, we think we will never love again. It wasn't long ago before the guy I just told you about came into my life, that I found myself in that familiar, unwanted place. When the love I had ended, I swore my heart would never mend and I would never love again. The motto of my life was that of an old popular song, you've probably heard it, who knows you probably even thought about it. It went like this *"in my life there's been heartache and pain, I don't know if I could take it again."* Funny thing, just when I loved again, Wynona Judd did a remake of that old Foreigner song. I must say, there had been other loves in my life that had come to an end before; other times when I thought I would not love again or my heart mend and I did and it did, but never like this. There was something different about this time. I had never, ever loved someone and given so much for so long. I thought the love I felt would last forever, I really thought it was a once in a lifetime, until death, do us part kind of love. When it was over for good, (remember we had broken up many, many times before) and my heart had been so torn apart, I just knew I would never give all of it again. I remember thinking and telling my girlfriends I will never love another man like I loved___ ___. I won't allow myself to. They laughed and said "yeah right!!!!!" I guess they had said that at some point in their lives, too, huh? . Either that or they knew better than I did the wonderful things the Lord had in stored for me. What you think?

My love for this man was so deep that the mere thought of someone taking his place, in my thoughts and let alone in my heart was unimaginable. Now by no means do I want to minimize or take for granted the love I felt for this man, for it was wonderful and as deep as I knew how to love. I am grateful for having had the time that I had with him and for the "love" I felt, but truth be told, what I felt really wasn't love, after all, how could it be when I really didn't know how to love.

Praise God, for my friends were right, God had such wonderful things in store for me, but first the love I felt had to end. The Lord knew it had to end so I could love him. You see, when I loved this man, I didn't know the love of God. He was not in my life, and I certainly was not living in his will, he sure was knocking though wanting to get in and wanting me to live right. He knew that as long as I felt the love I did, I wouldn't be right. The love I felt had to end, I Praise God for allowing it to happen and for giving me the strength to endure it, for when it ended, I let him in. I say Praise God because it was when I allowed him to enter my life and rule in my heart that I finally learned about his love. A love that is more pure than any other love one can know. I tell you girlfriend, you might think you "love", but not until you know God and have experienced His love can you really know what it is to love.

> *Beloved let us love one another, because love is from God; everyone who loves is born of God and knows God. Whoever does not love God does not know God, for God is love.*
>
> *1 John 4:7-8*

When I learned about love, real love, the one we have been talking about, the one described in Corinthians, I realized that what I one day thought was love, was really not. What I thought was love was not for it was not patient, it was not kind, it was arrogant and rude, it was resentful, it kept records of wrong doings and it ended. Finally, for the first time in my life, when I was not expecting it, when I was not looking for it and for sure when I was not wanting it, I learned about and experienced something more real than I ever had before. For once, I was not afraid, I felt safe and I did what I thought I'd never do again. Would you believe it—I loved again?

There is no fear in love, but perfect love casts out fear.
1 John 4:18

True and Forever Love

You have read about different types of love. So is there such a thing as true and forever love? I believe there is. In fact, I know there is. True love overcomes sensible, rational discussion and logic. It forgets former disappointment, assumptions and questions. It moves forward without ever looking behind. It does not seek its own way on the contrary it sacrifices for others, at the expense of self. It delights in the pleasure of another, even more so, than the pleasure of one's self. True love believes in the impossible because it is based on God, He with whom all things are possible.

I was very touched when I read an article about people who had lost their loved once many, many years ago and never remarried. I read in that article that Life has to end; love does not. Reading that touched my heart profoundly. How true it is, that Life has to end; love does not. Really even the bible tells us that love never ends. How beautiful to love that way, to know that your love is forever. It is for that reason that in a world where getting married and getting divorced is so easy, many when they lose their loved ones stay unmarried. After all how could they replace the person they loved so much, how could they have better memories?

True love, of course there's such a thing, only one and it lasts forever.

The Greatest Love of All

There is no greater love than this: the love that God showed us. When in spite of knowing our faults, and our sins, he sent his son, Jesus down from heaven, to a dirty place, to endure the cross, wash away our sins, save us and set you and me free.

God's love was revealed among us in this way: God sent his only Son into The world so that we might live through them, not that we loved God but that He loved us and sent his Son to be the atoning sacrifice of our sin.
1 John 4:9-10

The love of God is unimaginable, indescribable, incomprehensible, and incomparable; there is nothing in the world it can be likened to. It is the biggest thing there is. Greater than anything we will ever encounter, grasp or fathom is His love. It is higher than any mountain, deeper than any sea, wider than any ocean, and lower than any pit.

As I sit here writing about God's love, I can't help but to think of the movie *"The Passion of the Christ"* I just saw. Wow!!!!! There's been so much talk about that movie being violent, when in fact it was barely a glimpse of what happened to Jesus Christ. I just know that if you saw the movie you walked out of the theater not only in tears, but also with a greater knowledge of God's love for us. I say theater, because I don't think anyone would wait for this movie to come out on video. Think about Jesus' suffering in the movie. Think about the whipping he had to endure, of the nails being driven through his nails. Now think about God for a moment, and all that he had to bear. To watch his son in such horrific pain and to know it was necessary and he could do nothing. If you are a mother like me, you can relate, I mean when things happen to our children, it's hard to take; it hurts us even more so than it hurts them. To know that our father God had to endure his son's suffering. Is that not love?

I dare you to tell me that not the greatest love of all? Could you really say you know of a love that is better? I didn't think so.

Final Note

You have read much about love in this chapter. You have read what love is, and what it is not. In this chapter I shared about my own loves, the one I thought I would never get over and had to finally put behind me. I shared my own testimony about how I came to love again, something I thought I'd never do again, and once I did, I had to let go of that love. A love that once I was willing to let go, ultimately became my one true love. You have learned through my testimony that sometimes you just have to be willing to let love go for when you do, wonderful things that will happen. You have learned in this chapter that there is a "loving" and a "being in love" and there is a difference between them, also the big difference between "lust" and "love". I hope you paid close attention to the fact that your love should cost, and the right man will pay whatever the cost. Of course, there is such a thing as a true, forever love. Lastly, love could not be written about without writing about the "greatest love of all", the love of God, for it is not until you know His love that you will be able to love. It is my sincere desire that I have been used to show you "What is Love?"

Prayer

Heavenly Father, I release you to make me fall in love with you completely and for you to become my greatest love. Lord, help me to not wake up love before it is time and only after I have discovered the love you alone can give. Once I am filled with your love alone, prepare my heart to receive the love you have set apart for me. Father God, teach me to understand love, accept it, appreciate it, and to give it the way you would me to. Lord, set me free and allow me to let go of any ties, hurt, and memories of past loves. Help me to mend my broken heart and to not be afraid to love again and share my heart. Lord, when I have found real and true love with an earthly man, help me to treat it accordingly and not try to mold it into what I expect it to be. Help me to be completely selfless and willing to sacrifice. Father God, make me feel the kind of love that is flexible, patient, kind, hopeful and never failing, the kind of love that is not boastful, is not rude, is not self-seeking, or easily angered and does not keep record of wrong doing. Let this love always protect, always trust, and above all things let it always, always persevere. In Jesus' name, I pray. Amen.

9
You're All and Everything

You will have many relationships in your life. There's the relationship you will have with your parents, with your children either already or one day, there's the relationship with your brothers and sisters by relation, and your brothers and sisters in Christ. Of course there will be relationships with your coworkers, your girl friends and your boy friends in the world that are not yet saved and of course let's not forget the "boyfriends" and I don't mean friends who are boys. Please realize this, I promise you if you do, your life will be much easier and much better lived. Realize what? You might ask. Realize that of all the relationships you have, none and I do mean none will be more fulfilling than the relationship you have with your Lord. We have talked about many things so far in this book. We have talked much in this book about the woman, we have talked about the man, and we have talked about love, now we must talk about what should be the most important person in your Life. I'm talking about the Lord, the one that should be your all, and everything.

People Will Leave

When it comes to relationships, regrettably I have to tell you that people, especially men will come into your life and they will leave. Honestly, I think God designed it that way so that we will trust him and seek from only him. I don't know what your experience has been with people leaving, I have had some, the Lord, God though, has shown me time and time again how he will never leave and that all I need is him. Think about it, has he not shown you the same thing?

> *Give thanks to the Lord, for he is good, his love endures forever.*
>
> *Psalm 107:1*

Through all the relationships you have, you will experience many things through your relationships. There will be the relationships that will make you feel used, even abused to the point you will feel pain. If you are lucky you will feel joy through relationships that will enrich you and challenge you to be the best you can be. There will be those in which the people you are associated with will hold you accountable to doing the right thing. There will be relationships in which people will push you into doing the wrong thing. There will be times in your relationships when your soul will be torn, your heart will be broken, and your hopes and dreams will be shattered. There will be times when you will be made to feel so let down that you will want to curl up and die. There will be the times when you are encouraged, and given the lift you so desperately need. For purpose of this chapter let's focus on a relationship that comes to an end and what happens once it does.

How easy if we knew from the get go that not everyone who comes into your lives would stay. I once read that a person comes into your life for a reason, a season or a lifetime. How true that is. Well honey, let me give you a piece of advice if a man wants to leave. Let him leave. Do not go trying to make someone stay with you, who wants to leave. If the thought of leaving has entered his mind, it will only be a matter of time before he does. My dear, you do not need someone in your life that you need to baby or requires high maintenance or he'll leave. Come on....do you really want to live like that? Afraid that the guy you are with could just leave? A relationship like that will rob you of what God has for you. On the contrary a relationship with the Lord will bless you, it will set you free, it will make you feel loved and allow you to succeed and achieve. With all that said please understand that sometimes you just have to let people go.

The Gift of Good-Bye

Believe it or not, sometimes good-bye as much as it hurts is a bittersweet gift. It could be that a good-bye is exactly what it will take for you to finally turn to God and accept him as your Lord. As for me, it was not until the man I was involved with and in love with left, and caused me to cry many tears that I totally turned to God. Take it from someone who's been there, once you accept God and choose to have a relationship with him, and place him above all others your life will be restored; you will feel complete and seek from no one that which only he can give. Know this, your future is not tied to someone who wants to leave your life, that they want to leave is no accident. If God had wanted them to stay, by God they would have stayed, them leaving means God wants you for himself, and then at the right time will show you someone that is better for you. Recognize this, accept it, and by all means if the person you are with is, not wanting to stay, go ahead and say good bye.

They went out from us, but they did not belong to us; for if they had belong to us, they would have remained with us.

1 John 2:19

Girlfriend, something incredibly awesome will happen when you say good-bye to someone who no longer wants to be in your life. You will turn to God. You will get to know him and you will learn to be happy with him alone. Not only will you learn to be happy, but just then, he will manifest himself in so many people around you, you know that person that left, the one that said good-bye, well so many will come to take his place that you will have to remind yourself of him, because he will no longer be on your mind. I know! How do I know? I know because I lived through it myself. It took me a while to realize it but the person who said good-bye to me, really gave me a gift. I ask you--Are you not tired of going up and down the rollercoaster of hopes and false expectations? Are you not tired of having yet another relationship fall apart? Are you not tired of another promise broken, of another dream shattered? If so, say goodbye, accept it as a gift. Once you have run to God and his word, let them complete you and make you whole, most importantly know that he will never leave.

What Only He Can Do

So many women are mistaken in looking to a man to give them what life has robbed from them. Things like a father's attention and affection, a mother's love. Things that can only come from God. Let's be real here, Men are not God and they certainly cannot give you what you have been missing. Sadly, it's at the end of so many attempts at getting from men what only God can give, that we find out that only making God our Lord and Savior can we put an end to our wandering and suffering and the unrealistic expectations we have from men. There are times when a woman tries as she may cannot heal herself. There are times, that a woman even when she is married, her husband can't put together the pieces of her broken heart. It is then that a woman reaches to her Lord. It is in Him, that she will feel whole and finally be complete. A woman when she has become whole is changed forever. She will have a glow on her face, a shimmer in her eyes, a confidence in her stride and everyone will know there's something different about her life. Believe me when I say that there is no greater relationship in a woman's life than the relationship she experiences with her Lord. No other relationship will be more fulfilling or make her feel more complete.

I tell you it is in knowing your Lord that you will ultimately be fulfilled beyond anything else you will ever experience. It is in knowing your Lord that you will end the search for that "thing" that you have been for so long looking for. Once you know your Lord, and know that he is in control of your life and holds you in his everlasting, loving arms you will be healed from the scars left behind from every other relationship you have pursued or been involved in. Once you know the Lord, you will look at your scars in a different light, for they will no longer just be proof that you have been hurt, but they will also be proof that you have healed. Once you get to know him you will feel restoration in your heart and the renewing of your mind in a way you never imagined possible. Once you know him you will feel protection, faith & strength like you have never felt before. Having a relationship with the Lord will truly free you from having expectations of a man that can only be met by God, and that once not met by a man will disappoint you. So how do I know this you might wonder? I know this the same way I know everything else. I've been there, done that, I have a t-shirt. I myself have had those expectations from a man and when he has not met them, and have become disappointed. I had to turn to God. Glorrryyyyy, for I am now at a place where I have a relationship with him and boy what a difference that has made in my life. My Lord is my all and everything. I have released man and no longer expect from him the things I can only get from God. Because of that choice my whole life changed and I am no longer disappointed or brokenhearted. I tell you it's a beautiful place to be at. It is when you get to this place and you feel the unconditional love that your lord gives you that filling a void is no longer a need.

> Come to me all you that are weary and are carrying heavy burdens, And I will give you rest. Take my yoke upon you and learn from me; for I am gentle and humble in heart, and you will find rest for your Souls. For my yoke is easy and my burden is light.
> Matthew 28:28-30

The Greatest Love

Girlfriend, take it from me; you may think you have it all. You may think you have everything, and there is nothing you need but I've got news for you. If you do not know the Lord and his love you really have nothing. If you don't want to believe me, fine, believe famous, mega-bucks "have it going on" people who have said it, I'm quickly reminded of some "Dallas Cowboys" who gave their lives to the Lord, Deoine Sanders and Michael Irvin. I distinctly remember them saying "No house, position, amount of money, success, women—nothing can make you feel complete like having the Lord in your life., You will never find happiness and a more pure love than the one you will find in your Lord." I am sure they were talking about the kind of happiness that allows you to see past whatever is happening to you for you know that with the Lord, regardless of what happens there is a promise and he has made a way of escape for things to be better. In the midst of all that is life, when you are facing things that make no sense and you feel like giving up, how sweet it is to know that there is a God that has your best interest at heart. A God that will give you the love and strength to continue to march no man could.

Think about the kind of love that God offers, like I have already stated his love is unconditional, it is a love that is not dependent on what you have done, what you do, how you do it, or what you look like. Open up to the Lord and embrace him with all you have, I'm talking about your all, your heart, mind, body, soul and strength, a way you probably never have before. Do this and you will never want or need from another that which only comes from God.

You shall love the Lord, your God with all your heart, and with all your soul, and with all your mind.
Matthew 22:37

Don't get me wrong, I have already said that at the right time God will bring you someone. I'm talking about a person who he will manifest himself in, but first learn this lesson. It's one of the most important lessons you'll ever learn, that's if you haven't learned it yet. That's that absolutely no man I'll say that again absolutely no man can be everything you want him to be, especially whenever you want him to be it. Only God can be your all and everything. A man can be all that you have ever wanted, want and will ever want. You might feel that a man can satisfy your needs, and he might, for a while, at best for a moment but let me tell you something, no man, in fact no one you have a human relationship with will ever satisfy your needs like the touch of God can.

When you have a relationship with God and you really, really know him as your Lord, you will boldly proclaim his name. When you have a real relationship with your Lord you will wash his feet with your tears, raise your hands up high to worship him, and surrender your all to him. Girlfriend, get to know the Lord, get to know him because you want to know him not because you "have to". Want to know him because you realize all he has done for you, because of what he has delivered you from and for how he has changed you. Want to know him because of how he loves you. Want to know him because you ultimately want to become like him. Once you get to know him and have a relationship with him, when you spend time with him, share with him, and listen to him you will have found the greatest love of all.

God's Love for Women

There's no doubt about it, God loves us all, it doesn't matter if we are a man or a woman. Strangely though, there's just something special about us women that awakens a unique love inside of him that is unlike the love he has for men. As his beloved daughters we touch his heart, and instill in him an incredible sense of compassion for us. Now isn't that wonderful to know? A compassion that makes him look out for our best interests and takes care of our needs. The bible is filled with stories of women who touched the heart of God, and made him show compassion think about it, there's the story of Esther, Ruth, the woman of Samaria, the woman with the issue of blood, and the woman who was caught in the act of adultery.

I tell you once a woman has known the love of her Lord, she will not be desperate for the love of any other for in the Lord she will have found what she has been searching for. In him she will have found what for so long she has thirst and hunger for. Now this is not to say that knowing the Lord will fill every single void you have and whalah....eliminate the need of a man, oh no, the Lord designed us to not be alone, to have a partner and with needs that have to be physically met. So you see you will still want a man, but you will not need a man at least not like you thought you needed a man. The Lord knows that it is not good for one to be alone, after all, it was He who said it was not good for man to be alone and formed Eve, right? What I'm saying is: that knowing the Lord will eliminate that desperate need for physical affection and affirmation that so many women need and blindly seek. A woman who knows the Lord and makes him her all and everything knows that she can run into his arms at any moment. She knows that he is always there, that he will never leave her or forsake her. She knows that she can go through things and they will not be too much to bear because he has made her promises he will not break.

> *Jesus said to her "Everyone who drinks of this water will*
> *be thirsty again, but those who drink of the water I give*
> *them will never be thirsty again, The water that I will*
> *give will become in them a spring of water gushing up*
> *eternal life."*
>
> *John 4:14*

A woman, who knows the Lord and his promises, knows that He is always there to listen to her and give her words of wisdom. Most importantly a woman who knows the Lord knows that He is always the same not like the men she's known before who have always changed.

How easy life would be if women knew from the beginning that all they needed was God. For they would turn to Him and not count on anyone else. They would know that when times got hard He would be there to carry them through; they would have peace in place of anxiousness, impatience, worry and so many other things we women feel. If women only knew. There are so many women, who unknowingly need the miraculous touch of the Lord in their lives, and don't even know where to begin to find it. Let me tell you something, the Lord's touch, is something easily attained just for the asking. It's sad to see how because of lack of knowledge of what is missing in their lives, women try to attain material things such as money, a career, a position, a man, a husband. These things can never replace the touch of their Lord and will leave them feeling like something is missing and dissatisfied in the end. Now let me make something clear here, all these things are not bad, don't let anyone make you think that they are, they're really not. It's when we seek these things to get the satisfaction we can only get from God that they are bad and dangerous to us. I have already said it; everything without the Lord is nothing. These things are called idols, oh yes, and if you know anything about idols, you know that they are tools of deception used to mislead or deceive us into danger or the power of the enemy; in short it is bait. Funny thing about idols is that we allow the devil to use them against us; all the while we have no idea that we are being a victim of deception.

If you in spite of all your successes still feel empty, like there's something missing in your life, you have allowed the devil to use some idol against you, and you my dear have been deceived. If this is you, I have a suggestion for you, I'd like to suggest that you come to know my all and everything, the one who satisfied all my longings and made me whole. In case you don't know him, His name is Jesus and he so much wants to meet you and desires more than anything else that you make him your all and everything. He wants you to love him with all your heart, all your soul and all your might.

> *You shall love the Lord your God with all your heart, And all your soul and with all your might.*
> *Deuteronomy 6:5*

Jesus is called rightfully so, so many names, Redeemer, King of Kings, Lord of Lords, Savior, Son of God, Wonderful Counselor, Prince of Peace, Almighty Father, Comforter. Let him be all those things to you... He's a promise keeper, His voice is calm and soothing, His words are full of wisdom his arms are stretched wide to hold you, His ears are always opened to hear you. I tell you knowing Him and all He's about will leave you longing for nothing and will quench every thirst you have ever had. It's only when a woman has felt the touch of her Lord that she will no longer feel emptiness and like I already said, she will become complete and totally whole.

You must arrive to a point in your life where you seek God in everything; I am talking about everything.

In every situation, every circumstance, every encounter, the smallest thing whatever is good, and whatever is bad. It's when you seek God in everything and with passion that you will be expectant of him and that my dear is a wonderful thing

I remember when I found myself at this place, talk about seeking God in everything. I tell you, I would lose my keys and I would ask for God's help to find them, I would be looking for a parking space and I would ask Him for help finding a space, not only did I ask for his help, but I started thanking him for everything, weather it was good or bad. I remember one time, rushing to get home, I was speeding and drove right by a cop car parked on the side of the road, I knew for sure those lights were going to flash behind me any minute, well praise God, they didn't, guess what I said? Thank you, Lord! There was another time when I was having problems with my car, when I took it to the shop and they told me I had a bad battery that needed to be replaced and it would cost $50, I was happy and praised God, I said "Thank you Lord" cause it wasn't something that would cost me more.

Believe me if you do not fall in love with God, you will fall in and out of love with man after man and wonder what on earth is going on. Imagine how much easier life would have been and how much heartache you would have saved yourself from by just loving him. Choose not to fall in love with God and you will constantly strive for someone or something to fill a void that could only be filled by him. I tell you, your hole is God-sized and you will end up disillusioned and discontent every time you try to fill it with what is outside of God. A man will be able to fill that hole, and it will feel good, but never will he fill it completely.

Don't you think it's about time you to fell in love with your Lord and have the love affair of a lifetime with him?

Girlfriend, let me tell you something, having a love affair with your Lord, now that's a real love life, you have no idea. It's a love affair that will be more exciting with each passing day. It will grow stronger as you get to know him, because every day you will be falling deeper in love with him. It's kind of the other way around than it is with a man. A man you fall in love with and then love, while God, your Lord, you love and then fall in love with. Now, as in any other relationship no matter how great it is, our love affair with our Lord can become monotonous, boring and the flame go out. In order for that not to happen, we need to nurture our relationship with him, we need to keep his presence alive and fresh, we do this by spending time talking to him, and in his word everyday. It's the only way you'll get to know him, face it, if you don't get to know him; it will be hard to want to spend time with him and especially hard to love him. After all you don't spend time talking to someone you don't love do you?

So how do you talk to God? You talk to God through prayer. The time you spend talking to him is directly associated with how much you love him. Maximize on this time for the results are incredible. There's peace that passes understanding, unspeakable joy, and the reassurance that your future is secured in Him. The tone of voice in which you speak to your Lord needs to be something you take into account also. When you speak to Him, your voice should not only be soft, but it should be filled with love, passion, adoration and appreciation. Please do not think that you have to raise your voice up to the Lord for him to hear you. He will hear you when you have a sweet, soft voice towards him and will appreciate you talking to him softly just as much as if you were yelling. Now come on girlfriend let's be real, you you're your tone of voice changes when you talk to that special man in your life? Okay, so you don't think it does, that's alright, I didn't think mine changed either, but it did, and I bet yours does too. I remember my girls always knew when I was talking to the special man in my life. They would tell me they knew because my voice changed. Imagine that. My voice changing when I talked to a man.

In regards to speaking to God, know that only to Him could you bear all your heart and soul to. With that in mind, when you speak to him, be honest, and let it all out. I mean come on it's not like He doesn't know it already, he knows everything. What do you think that back in the Garden of Eden when God asked Adam "where art thou?" He didn't know where he was at? Of course He knew, it's just that He wanted Adam to take some time to think about where He was at and what he was doing, he just wanted him to tell him. Don't you think sometimes He's just like that with us?

God is our wonderful counselor and he will help us to make good choices and decisions. God is a rebuilder and restorer; He will put all the pieces of our lives back together again.

Once you start experiencing the presence of God in your life you will start to feel so many things, that you will not think about being alone or finding someone. Instead, you will begin to feel like you are loved, cherished and have in your life everything you'll ever need. When you really experience a relationship with God, you can't help but change. Of course, I mean the type of relationship where you listen as well as speak to God, you will enter into such deep intimacy where you won't know how to explain it but you will have changed. Your heart, your mind, your soul, your life will be different. Everyone will know that you my dear have a love life for they will notice a difference in you and know that you are in love.

Draw near to God, and he will draw near to you.
James 4:8

Think about the Lord for a moment, think about all he is. He is a wonderful counselor; he will help you to make good choices and decisions. He is a rebuilder and restorer, he will put all the pieces of your lives together. Now think about all he has done for you. Think about all he has brought you through. That question reminds me of one of my favorite worship songs. It goes like this: when I think about the Lord, how he raised me, how he saved me, how he picked me up and turned me around how he placed my feet on solid ground. It makes me want to shout. Hallelujiah!!!!!Thank you Jesus!!!!

The Beginning

Beginning a relationship with the Lord, is just that: a beginning. It will take time to get to know Him. Like other relationships you will have you will have to work on this one, it will not just happen. Oh no, you will have to invest big time. I tell you though, no other investment will give you a greater return. You will realize as you invest time in Him, learning about Him, talking to Him and listening to Him, that he will become your best friend. You will see that the more you know Him the more and more He will mean to you with each passing day. You will begin to give Him more and more of you. One day the Lord God will be your, everything and you will give Him everything. I'm telling you that day you will have hit the "jackpot".

Please understand that beginning a relationship with the Lord does not mean that you will never be attacked again and that adversity will just fade away. Your life will not suddenly be perfect, but starting a relationship with Him is the beginning.

I Am Who I Am

God said to Moses I AM WHO I AM.
                                    Exodus 3:14

God says in his word "I Am Who I Am". You might ask "I Am", "I Am" who? I am what? Well do I have an answer for you, you see my dear, God is anything and everything, whatever you need him to be, whenever you need him to be it, he's even what you have no idea you need. I don't know about you but to me that's mind boggling to know. No one else, absolutely no one can be this; I'm talking about anything and everything you need. Many may come close but I tell you, no one can be it. No doubt about it, God's "the man". My dear sister, check this out, the Lord, he is your husband, your lover, your friend, your provider, you confidant, your counselor, your protector, your ever-present help in time of need, once you know him, I mean really know him there will be no one or nothing else you will need. God is loving, he is faithful, generous, caring, and thoughtful, he is merciful, sensitive, wise, compassionate, forgiving, and strong, he is a man like no other, or have you ever met a man like that? A man who keeps his promises and never lies. Now isn't that everything you want in a man? So what are you waiting for? Start a new life right this minute; fall in love with the Lord and make him

"Your All and Everything".

Final Word

It was absolutely wonderful to write such a chapter. I just love to write about the Lord. He has been so good to me, and showed me so much grace. He is the love of my life, the hope that I cling to, he means more than this world to me. I wouldn't trade him for silver and gold, I wouldn't trade him for treasures untold, and I love to share him. To him, be the glory for he has worked wonders in my life. I am what I am because he entered my life and poured blessings unto it. I have written about many topics in this book. Of all, I would have to say that this chapter on the Lord is one of the most if not the most important chapter in this book. Life will teach you many lessons, as you have already learned, but it is in learning about God, knowing Him, and letting Him be your Lord that you have learned the most important lesson of them all. By learning it you have the foundation in place for everything else you have read about. It is my desire that through this reading that you have come to know God better, that you have fallen in love with Him, and that you have made the biggest decision of your life to make Him "Your all and everything".

Prayer

    Heavenly Father, Thank you for all that you are and all that you have done in my life. I love you so much and in you have found the peace I have never before known. Forgive me Lord, for the time I didn't know you and sought in other men, what I could only find in you. Thank you Lord for leading me to you. Thank you Lord, for being my all and everything. Thank you for salvation and deliverance, thank you for touching my heart the way that only you could. Lord, I thank you for so many things, I especially thank you for your presence and making me feel complete, for without you I would feel empty and I would have nothing. Lord, I just give you all the honor, glory and praise for you alone are worthy, only you have satisfied all my wants and have given me strength to seek from only you what only you can give. I ask you Lord, to continue to reside in me, and grow in me, quench any thirst or hunger that I may have, any need I may feel I need. I ask all these things in the mighty name of Jesus. Amen.

10
The Best is Yet to Be

We sometimes live our lives so into the present, or still dwelling on the past that we hold no regard for the future and how wonderful it can be. Once we become saved and choose to live as Christians, we come to the realization that everything we have lived and endured were, steps ordered by God. Steps necessary to get us to where we are and direct us towards the future He has always purposed us to live. What a joy it is to know that we do not have to live with fear in our lives of the future for the Lord has His hands on it. When the future belongs to Him, all you have to do is know that you can depend on him. At the end, when you are blessed to have lived a long life you will have seen the past unfold before you and know why some things just had to be. Till then rise up, look at life straight in the face, expect and declare boldly with all your strength "The Best is Yet to Be."

It's Not Over

Have you any idea that God is preparing you very carefully and patiently for your destiny? He is. Have no doubt about it, you are a work in progress, constantly being molded and refined to achieve his purpose. A purpose that is wonderful and specifically designed with you in mind. In the end, you will see that you are a designed masterpiece and will serve a purpose only you can serve because it was planned for you long before your past. Believe me when I tell you, your life is not over—just because you have been through some stuff. The pain, the hurt, the betrayals, doesn't mean your life is over. Remember we talked about things happening for a reason early on. Girl, whatever you've been through, it's all in the past, say that and believe it in Jesus' name. In Jesus' name you have a future and the best is yet to be. Hallelujah, I know that's right! God did not bring you through all the stuff he brought you through so that you could just get to heaven. Oh no honey, it's not going to be that easy. He brought you through all he did so that you could be a walking testimony to those around you, so you can show them what it means to be blessed and so you could live the future that was designed for you.

Surely there is a future, and your hope will not be cut off.
Proverbs 23:18

Have no doubt your future is going to be wonderful. I promise you it will be, I can promise you it will be cause God has already promised you it would be, and He won't let you down. He can't because he cannot lie. He's bound by the promise he has made and He will do what He said He would do in your life.

An Everyday Thing

Living for the future, is pretty much an everyday thing that you have to take day by day. That means that everyday you live--is for it. It means you have to start living for your future today. Sometimes we wait thinking we will start to live our lives one day and sadly, allow the drive and anxiousness for it, prevent us from living in the present and savoring life everyday.

We actually determine our future by what we do in the present and how we handle things that happen to us while we are in it. In other words, our future is shaped everyday, so it is now. That's right it starts now not later, don't you think for a minute that you have time to waste, for every moment you waste now is really a moment you can have later. So, make the best of every moment knowing that it is propelling you into the future. I remember years ago, I worked with a company in an industry where retention was very challenging. People constantly left from one company to the next because of the sign on bonus and incentives. Well, my company came up with a brilliant idea. It went like this: anything you commissioned one quarter, if you were with the company at the end of the quarter a year later, you would get a bonus check in the amount of your commissions again. I'm talking thousands and thousands of dollars. Imagine that, I was not only working for that year, but the next year as well. I was so psyched I worked so hard, and made lots of money. I believe that was the year when I made the most money. Isn't it funny, how our attitudes change when we know there is something in it in the future? Well honestly, is there anything better than your future? I don't think so.

Make no mistake about it; you were on the mind of God long before you were born. In fact God thought of you before you were knitted in your mother's womb. That means you were on his mind even before you were in your past. Deep, huh? Well check this out; you were in the future before you were in your present. Remember that only God knows your, yesterday, today and tomorrow all in one glance. So, it is for your future that you have lived all you have lived in your past, and what you are living in the present, what you live tomorrow—what you live everyday.

An Attitude of Gratitude

When I think about my life and my future, all I can say to the Lord is "I am amazed". I am truly amazed at what His love has done for me, so much that I have to smile and say, "thank you". My God has been sooooo good to me; I tell you even my mess he blessed, I just can't help but have an attitude of gratitude. All I can do is be thankful to the Lord, my attitude of gratitude will never cease, and praise will continuously be on my lips.

So much I have gone through and many battles I have fought. I thought I had lost many battles, only to get to the future and realize, I had not lost them at all, but won them. I am sure the same goes for you. You will get to the future and see why you went through things you did and just like me, you will say "thank you"!

I promise you that the things that are ahead of you will justify all the things behind you, believe me, even if you cannot see it right now, they will. I remember having Thanksgiving Day get-togethers in my home. I started a tradition where we would all stand in a circle, hold hands, and give thanks out loud for something in our lives. I thanked the Lord for all the battles he gave me to fight and for the people who were only in my life for a season and were no longer there. I was thankful for everything

I went through. I didn't know it then but The Lord was working on me.

I just know that the Lord has something wonderful in store for me, but if he didn't do anything else for me, I would be thankful for all he has already done and praise Him anyway.

> *I am confident of this, that the one began a good work among you will bring it to completion by the day of Jesus Christ.*
>
> *Philippians 1:6*

Know that although you went through things and sometimes wondered what was going on, your Lord, God always knew. That's right, he knew what was going on and how He was going to get you through it. While you were going on and struggling with your daily life, God was playing chess with it and was waiting for that opportune time to make his move and proclaim, "checkmate"! So the next time something happens in your life, that you don't think you'll get through, reach deep down inside of you and remind yourself of what God has done for you in the past. Remember that he has delivered you from so much, so that you my dear could have a future.

Let God Drive

I tell you girlfriend, only when you are happy, in your present state and start to live in it will you receive, the gift of the future, God has for you. Make no mistake about it; God will not give you things before then. Please do not live your life trying to change what is, so much that you never get to see what could be. You have been down many roads, been slowed down by bumps and have gotten lost more times than you can't count. Get the drift you obviously cannot drive so don't go trying to be in the driver's seat in your life. Move over and let God take the wheel, only he can drive. Once you decide to let Him drive, accept where you are at and never lose sight of where you are going—towards a beautiful future. Begin living for tomorrow today and make it last a lifetime through.

In the Future

There will come a day when you will see that everything you lived in the beginning was so that you could have a better future. Trust me, one day you will see that the future and the wonderful things that are happening in it, are the end result of everything you have lived. The end will be better than the beginning; you can take that to the bank.

> *Remember the former things of old; for I am God and there is no other; I am God and there is no one like me, declaring the end from the beginning.*
> *Isaiah 46:9-10*

Now, to have the type of future that is better than the beginning, you will have to do things differently, you will have to stop the insanity. By insanity, I mean doing the same thing over and over again and expecting different results. I know you know what I'm talking about; I mean many of us have been there. I know I was what you could call "insane". I say that for such was my life. I would do things over and over again, expecting different results. There's a saying that goes if you keep doing what you've always done; you will keep getting what you've always had. Why I thought things would be different was beyond me. Praise God, I got my sanity back; back before it was permanently damaged.

I'd like to teach you some things about your life in the future. First thing is that in the future all (and I do mean all) the dreams God has given to you will come to past. Rest assured God would not put something in you and then not give you what it takes to make it happen. Oh noo-sery!!!!!! However satisfying your life is here on earth, the best is yet to be. That's right, when it is all said and done you my dear will arise. Believe me God has designed a future for you and you for that future. He has put something in you for you to use in the future that no one else can.

He will wipe every tear away from their eye. Death will be no more; Mourning, and crying and pain will be no more, For the first things have passed away.
Revelation 21:4-5

Have I made it plain? Can you see that the future and the destiny God has planned for you is so much greater than where you are at today? I'd be willing to bet that your present is greater than your past. Right? Based on that historical fact, wouldn't it stand to reason that your future is going to be greater than your present? I know that's how life has been for me. My life has gotten better as the years have gone by. Things have come to pass. Think about your own life, has it not gotten better through the years? Because of that I know the best is yet to be. I wait both patiently and anxiously at the same time for it. I do not fear for I know that it is for the future that I have lived all I have lived in the past, and all I live in the present.

See, the former things have come to pass, and new things I Now declare; before they spring forth, I tell you of them.
Isaiah 42:9

217

For Such a Time as This

I have begun to live the incredible life, the Lord always purposed me to live. My life right now is the happiest it has have ever been. I feel so blessed; I'm blessed so abundantly, that my cup runneth over. I just know that everything—absolutely everything that I have lived has been for such a time as this.

Your eyes beheld my unformed substance. In your book were written all the days that were formed for me, when none of them as yet existed.
Psalm 139:16

Soon I will start to plan my wedding. It's going to be beautiful, like a dream come true. Even more beautiful than the wedding will be the life that will follow it. A wonderful husband, wonderful children, ministry, an even deeper relationship with the Lord almighty. You see, where two or more are gathered, He is right there in the midst. Isn't that wonderful?

Funny thing, sometimes you have to be careful of what you wish for. For you might just get what you wish for. I always thought (wished) that I would want to cry on my wedding day, when it was time to say our vows. You see, when that time came, I didn't want traditional vows spoken by a pastor, oh no, I wanted to pour out my heart to my future husband in front of witnesses (many of which knew much of what I had gone through). I knew I would want to tell him, how much he meant to me, how he was a gift, how much I loved and appreciated him. I wanted tears of joy to flow from my eyes. Tears of joy, knowing that I had gone through much in my life to get to that point I was at, and was so happy for it. I have no doubt that when that time comes, I will definitely cry. You see, I had some tough times in my life, I have cried many tears of sadness, I have felt much pain, and had someone walk out on me that made me doubt I would ever, ever have better days. So you see, on that day, my wedding day, I will know all it took, for me to feel that way, I will appreciate everything that I have and be thankful for everything that had to take place.

> But it is written, "what no eye have seen, no ear heard, nor the human heart conceived, what God has prepared for those who love Him.
> *1 Corinthians 2:9*

All Worth It

Praise God for He knew what He had in store for me. He knew that my end was going to be so much better than my beginning. He knew that there would come a day when I would look back on my life, and I would say "for such a time as this". Everything, in my life, the good, the bad, the ugly, absolutely everything justified who and where I was at the moment. Believe me, everything has been worth it, even if I had a chance to do it all again, I would not change a thing. The happiness I feel today, so much makes up for the hurt I felt yesterday. My life has become a fairy tale, with a prince and all.

Think about your own life for a moment. It could be that soon or years from now, someday in the future you will find yourself at a place where you will realize that where you are at and every place you have been to is to get you to a certain place. You too, will see and one day say it was all worth it. Let me let you in on a secret, "I should have known that my Lord God, who loves me so much, did not bring me through all He did just to leave me". Oh no, and I know now more than ever that as good as my life is, "The Best is yet to Be"!

Final Word

I knew writing a chapter about the future would take me no time. I guess cause there's not much to say about the future, after all, it is the future, it has not yet happened. Right? Well, I can say this about it--it's starting to look awesome. Better and greater than everything I have lived. I must say that of all the chapters in this book, this last one has been the shortest and easiest to write. Short and easy however are not the only words to describe this chapter, for I found it to be refreshing and inspiring. It had brought joy to my life and a feeling of expectancy. I'd like for you to think the same thing about your own future. Be refreshed, inspired, full of joy and expectant. Seriously, if there was one thing I would want you to take from this chapter is to know that you have a future and be expectant that part of that future is that "The Best is Yet to Be"!

Prayer

Heavenly Father, I thank you right now for my future, and all the decisions I have made and am yet to make that will lead me to it. I thank you Lord because you are the center of my life and have all my days in your hands. Your word says that no eyes have seen, no ears have heard, nor the human heart conceived what you have prepared for those who love you. Lord God, I stand firm on your promises you have made to me; promises that say that surely I have a future and my hope will not be cut off; that I can be confident that you who began a good work in me are faithful to complete it. Father God, I have no fear of things being so good, that they will turn bad, like they always use to, for I deserve the goodness that you are pouring on my life. I have cried many tears in my past and am merely reaping a harvest from all I have sown. I plea the blood of Jesus over my life and use my authority to tell the devil that he will not have his way in it, that I was born to be a victor and a victim like I have been in the past I will no longer be. Lord, I ask that you use everything in my past in the future to give others hope and inspire them to be what you purposed them to be. I ask all these things in your precious son, Jesus' name. Amen.

A Final Word

Two years went by from the time I started writing this book, till the time I was done. Wow, what two years they had been! The year I started writing was the worst year of my life while the year I finished would undoubtedly be my best year. I thank God; to Him be the glory. He has been soooooooo good to me!!!! I have done so much growing and changing during this time. My inner self went through total reconstruction. The pieces of my shattered heart were put together, my soul was renewed. My outer self seemed to have gone through reconstruction itself, for I now glowed with an inner beauty and happiness I had never before known.

My whole life flourished during the writing of this book. I reconciled with my past and was delivered from it, I forgave, I said good-bye, and I realized my worth. I practiced excellence, learned discernment, and began to live in purity and righteousness. I became involved in serving, ministry work and church leadership. I began to thank God for everything and prayed about everything. While our country was going through a recession and so many people were losing their jobs and their homes, my career and my finances suffered a bit, but compared to so many were still intact. I settled into a beautiful home, overwhelmed with peace and warmth I had never before felt. My relationships blossomed and blessed me in so many ways. My relationship with my daughters and my parents became better. I became great friends with women the Lord brought into my life for me to be mentored by and to minister to. Most Importantly, my relationship with God and my walk with Him reached a deeper level. As if that wasn't enough, just when I had given up on feeling things I had felt before, God gave me the gift of a wonderful Godly man for me to become best friends with, who challenged me to grow, and taught me to love again.

For as long as I can remember, I have enjoyed reading. As a young girl I spent hours and hours in the library with my head glued to books. I read to my girls so much, that by the time my oldest was four years old, she picked up The Three Little Pigs and blew me away when she read It to me as I had to her so many times. I had given some thought to writing a book when I was younger and in the world. I mean, I had lived a wild, kind of exciting, juicy, interesting life. The kind of life that is written about and movies are made of. Needless to say my idea of a book was more along the lines of the "Hollywood Wives" kind of story. Never did I think about a Christian-based book with scriptures and prayer, oh no, not at all. God though, had a plan for my life and wanted me to use my wild, kind of exciting, juicy, interesting life for his glory. He knew that what I had experienced could help others and gave me the desire and passion to put it in form of this book.

Without a doubt, the Lord commissioned me to write this book. I thank him for His marvelous ways. I thought I had so much information in me. I mean I had lived through a lot, of course I could help others. I thought I knew about women and I knew about men. I had a saying that went like this: "everything in life, I have done, or it has been done to me, I know someone who has done it or who it has been done to". I didn't realize that I still had a lot to learn and that I needed help. Then I came to know God, boy did He teach me about him, faith, forgiveness, patience, about letting go of the past, intimacy, adversity, love, being single and the future. Oh yes and about women and men. Little did I know that along with the many women I would minister to and help through this book, I would minister to and help myself and because of it become a better woman.

Today, I am in a place where I am in love with God. I am happy, content, full of life and very much looking forward to the future. I am presently preparing for so many things, in the very near future I will be marrying the wonderful man God brought to my life—a year and a half ago, the man who became my best friend. I am so excited about sharing my life with him. Of course I don't know all about my future and I have questions. Question like: How good will this book do? Will I be a vessel for the Lord and travel around the country to speak about what I have written? Will I minister with my husband? Will I live to see generations of my life be blessed? Will I leave behind a legacy? I do not have all the answers or know exactly what the future holds but I have allowed God's will and not mine to be done in my life. I just know that with The Lord's guidance and the love I have beside me, the best is yet to come.

I give all the praise, honor and glory to God for He alone is worthy. He took my life, turned it upside down, took people out of it and opened up the windows of heaven to pour out wonderful blessings over it. I love my life; it is absolutely awesome. Better than all my dreams. What's really wonderful is the fact that yesterday I suffered and yesterday I cried, but "*Today, I Cry No More!*"

About The Author

Marianela Olivas is a very involved on fire leader in Shoreline's Christian Center Singles' Ministry in Austin, Texas. She enjoys traveling, reading, writing and speaking. She has spoken to Women and Singles. Her desires are to be a Godly mother to her beautiful daughters, Nichole and Bianca, to leave a legacy, to be a wonderful wife to the wonderful man God has brought into her life, and to speak, teach and minister to hurting women.

Printed in the United States
57725LVS00001B/145-228